TRUTH
THAT SETS
AMERICA
FREE

To Paul
for God & America
Prov 14:34

7-31-18

TRUTH
THAT SETS
AMERICA
FREE

RANDY HEKMAN

Truth That Sets America Free
Copyright © 2012 by Randall J. Hekman

ISBN 978-0-9854134-0-8

Editor: Dave Lambert
Cover design: Rob Monacelli
Interior design: Beth Shagene

Printed in the United States of America

12 13 14 15 16 17 • 10 9 8 7 6 5 4 3 2 1

*I dedicate this book to my best friend
and wife of forty-three years, Marcia,
who has been an amazingly courageous example
of what a true follower of Christ should be.*

"Then you will know the truth,
and the truth will set you free."
(John 8:32)

"There is a way that appears to be right,
but in the end it leads to death."
(Proverbs 14:12)

Contents

Preface | 11

Acknowledgments | 15

1 The Liberating Power of Truth | 17

2 Government: All or Nothing? | 31

3 Liberty: God's Gift or Man's Creation? | 55

4 Civil Society That Works | 77

5 Christian Citizenship 101 | 97

6 Transforming Welfare — a Triple Win | 119

7 My Life for Your Life | 149

About the Author | 165

A Special Note from the Author's Wife | 167

Preface

I WRITE THIS BOOK WITH A HEAVY HEART BECAUSE my beloved nation America is on an extremely perilous course. I want to see her rescued before it is too late.

As a follower of Christ, I totally understand that no nation lasts forever, and we are commanded in Scripture to set our mind and hearts on things above, not on things of this earth (Colossians 3:1-2). I seek daily to do exactly that. But I love the idealism of America, our heritage of wanting to do the right thing, to be honorable and willing, if need be, to face evil aggressors and help those in need. In the history of the world, there has been no other nation like America. I love her as you would love a faithful friend.

I don't wish to sugarcoat our history, nor suggest that there have not been many problems and failures along the way. The biggest may have been slavery and the Civil War, both of which leave a major blot on our national record.

But despite these disgraces and scores of other short-comings, Americans through the years have done about as well as a group of fallible humans could do in establishing a nation founded on the radical idea of self-government — government of the people, by the people, and for the people. And that truly has been the secret of our success: turning self-governing people free to succeed or fail — and if they fail, encouraging them to get up and try again and again until their efforts meet success. God has wired greatness into each of us. America has provided a fertile setting for that greatness to come out and bless others.

But all of that is about to end. As we recount in this book, little by little, America has forsaken the principles that produced its success. We now minimize the creative contributions of free citizens and magnify the value of our central government. Accompanying the unprec-edented growth of government has been debt growing at a rate that virtually all experts agree is unsustainable. We are moving toward an economic meltdown that will make the current problems in Greece appear mild by compari-son. Time is running out to deal with the problem. How it will impact you and your family is not certain. But what is certain is that it *will* impact you and your family.

The symptoms of this growing crisis are the growing ocean of red ink and frustrating gridlock in Washington, but the actual source of the problems comes from every corner of America. Government reflects culture. Government is sick because culture is sick. The cure for a sick culture has always been the same: we need God. We are neither smart enough nor good enough to figure our way out of this morass without him. We need to seek him and earnestly pray that we as a people will turn back to the one who has been and remains the Best Friend our nation has ever had. There simply is no other way, no other shortcut to bring healing to America.

We can do this. But it will take all of us doing our part. If we do, who knows but that God in his mercy will give America one more opportunity to experience his blessing and, again, to be a source of blessing to the world.

Acknowledgments

WHILE MY NAME APPEARS ON THIS BOOK AS ITS author, this book itself and the quality of my very life are the result of the contributions of thousands of relatives, friends, and others who have helped me become who I am and to know what I believe. God is the Grand Orchestral Conductor of all that, and therefore I wholeheartedly thank him for what he has done to allow and enable me to share my heart and mind with you in written form. That is truly a blessing.

On the human plane, I would be remiss in not thanking each of our twelve children (Michelle, Renee, Alicia, Marianne, David, Suzanne, John, Scott, Laurie, Daniel, Angela, and Nathan) for showing me vividly the inestimable value of each individual person created by an amazingly wise God. While all our kids share a similar "Hekman" look, each is incredibly unique and special. I am so blessed to know each one!

For teaching me so many of life's lessons, I'm indebted to my parents, John and Mary Lou Hekman, who are now with the Lord. Thanks too for my awesome sisters, Barbara Mengebier, Jane DeGroot, and Manette DeJonge, for their love for me and support along the way.

I'm grateful to our pastor Rod VanSolkema, who has taught me so much about loving God with my whole heart. I also am grateful for some of the best campaign staff people in the world. Currently helping me are: Kurtis Fowler, Chris duMond, Darlene Kolehouse, and Teresa LaHaie. Other wonderful men and women have served on my staff in the past: Ryan King, Jim Hossler, Kristin Kolehouse, Mark Roth, and Tim Beals.

The talented and godly folks at Somersault Group, John Topliff and Dave Lambert, are professionals who really know their craft. It's been a joy working with them.

Finally, I thank my best friend and wife of forty-three years, Marcia, for her love and patience with me and her daily encouragement to be all God has made me to be. I love her more than I can describe.

1

The Liberating Power of Truth

THE STORY OF THE UNITED STATES OF AMERICA IS nothing short of phenomenal. In less than two hundred years, we grew from a loose-knit grouping of fledgling colonies to become the richest and most powerful nation in the history of the world. While we endured times of great testing, including the Revolutionary War, the Civil War, and the two major world wars, we emerged from each of these struggles stronger and more unified. Throughout our history, we have granted incredible economic opportunity and overwhelming personal freedoms to millions of our citizens. We have allowed immigrants from virtually every place on earth the opportunity to become part of this wonderful experiment in liberty and opportunity.

Consider this: while the U.S. comprises only 5 percent of the world's population, we have nonetheless created more new wealth than the rest of the world combined. We have never endured a famine; in fact we have been the breadbasket to the world. Our inventions and discoveries have revolutionized health care, transportation, agriculture, manufacturing, the digital revolution, and national defense. At the same time, Americans have shown incredible heart and generosity — we are always the first to respond with relief to nations suffering from natural disaster, pestilence, and the ravages of war.

What is the secret of America's phenomenal success?

Some might suggest that it's the ethnic makeup of our people. But there must be more to it than that, since the United States' ethnic makeup is nearly impossible to define: we are a melting pot, with many nationalities and races. Perhaps our success is due to the abundance of our natural resources. We are truly blessed with much in that regard, but not nearly enough to reasonably explain the amazing nation we have become.

I firmly believe that America became the greatest nation in the history of the world because our framers, the courageous and gifted people who created the philosophical and political framework for the United States, established a civil society that allows people the freedom to choose to be all that God made them to be. Our founders believed in the inestimable value of each individual life and allowed this conviction to permeate every part of our political and legal system. This liberty enshrined in law has allowed ordinary Americans to take risks, and often through even repeated failures, to persevere and ultimately create the wealth, art, music, literature, and inventions that have blessed not only them and their families, but the rest of our nation and the entire world.

> I believe the evidence is overwhelming that our framers discovered and expertly applied the "operating instructions" for making a civil society that promotes growth and liberty. Simply put: They founded the nation on absolute truth.

The question remains: *Where* did our framers obtain the wisdom to launch so successful a nation? I believe the evidence is overwhelming that our framers discovered and expertly applied the "operating instructions" for making a civil society that promotes growth and liberty. Simply put: They founded the nation on absolute truth. Jesus put it this way: "Then you will know the truth, and the truth will set you free" (John 8:32).

The major premise of this book is: *Truth works*. I

believe there are truthful principles consistent with God's design of the universe that, when embraced, promote liberty and life itself. The opposite of that is also true: When we don't embrace the truth, we inexorably move away from liberty toward enslavement and ultimate death. This reality applies not only for individuals but for families and nations as well.

Truth has taken a beating in our day. According to a Barna survey, only about one-third of Americans believe in the existence of moral absolutes anymore. Even among those who consider themselves "born again," less than half of respondents acknowledged a belief in moral absolutes. Why is this significant? Because, without moral absolutes, without a belief that there is an objective standard of morality that is absolutely true, each person gets to define for himself or herself what is truly right and wrong.

> Even secular scholars have documented that the Bible was the most frequently quoted background source between 1760 and 1805 by those who had a hand in shaping our nation.

The people who founded our nation believed in absolute truth and error. In contrast to our modern relativistic thinking, in which religious and moral ideas are generally relegated to the category of *opinion*, the framers were willing to stake their lives on their philosophical convictions, which they viewed as solidly, absolutely *true*. The Declaration of Independence shows how strongly they believed in these convictions:

When in the Course of human events, it becomes necessary for one people to dissolve the political bands which have connected them with another, and to assume among the powers of the earth, the separate and equal station to which the Laws of Nature and of Nature's God entitle them, a decent respect to the opinions of mankind requires that they should declare the causes which impel them to the separation. —

We hold these truths to be self-evident, that all men are created equal, that they are endowed by their Creator with certain unalienable Rights, that among these are Life, Liberty and the pursuit of Happiness. — That to secure these rights, Governments are instituted among Men, deriving their just powers from the consent of the governed, — That whenever any Form of Government becomes destructive of these ends, it is the Right of the People to alter or to abolish it, and to institute new Government, laying its foundation on such principles and organizing its powers in such form, as to them shall seem most likely to effect their Safety and Happiness....

And for the support of this Declaration, with a firm reliance on the protection of Divine Providence, we mutually pledge to each other our Lives, our Fortunes, and our sacred Honor.

So what was the sourcebook for the framers' wisdom in setting up our nation? How did they figure out the operating instructions for what was to become the most successful nation in the world? The evidence is clear. The framers repeatedly sought advice and counsel from the age-old wisdom contained in divine Scripture, the Bible. Even secular scholars have documented that the Bible was the most frequently quoted background source between 1760 and 1805 by those who had a hand in shaping our nation.[*] Contrary to revisionists' theories of our founding, almost half of the signers of the Declaration of Independence had the equivalent of seminary or Bible school degrees.

With gratitude to David Barton and his WallBuilders organization[†], here's just a sampling of the relevance our

---

[*] Donald Lutz, The Origins of American Constitutionalism, 1988, 136–149.
[†] See http://www.wallbuilders.com.

founders attributed to the Bible in helping shape what was to become the United States of America:

John Jay, coauthor with Alexander Hamilton and James Madison of the Federalist Papers and first chief justice of the U.S. Supreme Court:

> The Bible is the best of all books, for it is the word of God and teaches us the way to be happy in this world and in the next. Continue therefore to read it and to regulate your life by its precepts.*

John Adams, signer of the Declaration of Independence, second president of the U.S.: "I have examined all religions, and the result is that the Bible is the best book in the world."†

Benjamin Rush, signer of the Declaration of Independence:

> [T]he only means of establishing and perpetuating our republican forms of government is the universal education of our youth in the principles of Christianity by means of the Bible.‡

---

*William Jay, *The Life of John Jay* (New York: J. & J. Harper, 1833), Vol. II, 266, to the Rev. Uzal Ogden on February 14, 1796.

†John Adams, Works, Vol. X, 85, to Thomas Jefferson on December 25, 1813.

‡Benjamin Rush, *Essays, Literary, Moral & Philosophical* (Philadelphia: Thomas & Samuel F. Bradford, 1798), 112, "A Defence of the Use of the Bible as a School Book."

Noah Webster, revolutionary soldier, judge, "Schoolmaster to America":

[O]ur citizens should early understand that the genuine source of correct republican principles is the Bible, particularly the New Testament, or the Christian religion.*

Drawing on the teachings of Scripture, our framers were able to understand, at least as far as finite minds can, God's order in the universe and the work of his sovereign hand not only in establishing the physical realm and natural laws, but in creating man, endowing him with rights, and instructing him to heed the moral laws that are also part of the universe. While the Bible describes man as being created in the image of God, it also taught our framers about man's fallen nature and his tendency toward selfishness and greed. So while our framers wanted to allow free people to use their talents for good, they also understood the necessity of a criminal justice system to maintain order. And, because leaders are also fallen and subject to sin, our founders intentionally instituted the separation of powers and checks and balances in the governmental structure to limit the ability of any leader to

---

* Noah Webster, *History of the United States* (New Haven: Durrie and Peck, 1832), 6.

usurp authority and create tyranny. Our framers also spoke much about the need for all citizens to possess self-government, whereby each of us govern ourselves due to our commitment to God and conscience. That alone allows government to grant liberty to its citizens without anarchy ensuing. John Adams put it this way:

> [W]e have no government armed with power capable of contending with human passions unbridled by morality and religion.... Our constitution was made only for a moral and religious people. It is wholly inadequate to the government of any other.*

Again, my premise is that truth works, and, for America, truth *did* work, and it worked very well.

So why the need for this book? It is obvious to most Americans in our day that America's growth and greatness has stalled out. Our out-of-control national debt, unemployment, economic stagnation, gridlock in Washington, soaring crime, family disintegration, and a general sense of national hopelessness have taken over.

As I have studied the problems we face, I would say that, if anything, most Americans don't know the half

---

*John Adams, *The Works of John Adams, Second President of the United States,* Charles Francis Adams, editor (Boston: Little, Brown, and Co. 1854), Vol. IX, 229, October 11, 1798.

of the serious issues we face as a nation. Should trends continue, we are truly within a handful of years of experiencing catastrophic economic collapse like those we see across the ocean with debt-saturated nations like Greece, Italy, and Spain. Like a bad dream in which we find ourselves moving inexorably toward disaster, America is heading toward a cliff with seemingly nothing to stop our motion.

I did not write this book to be a source of discouragement. In fact, it's just the opposite — I want to promote hope and healing. Like the framers of our nation and many of you readers, I believe in the power of truth to liberate and give life. I've seen it in my own life and that of my family. But, for our nation to reap the benefits of truth, the first step we will need to take is to face the reality of the crisis we are in. Then we will need to determine the source of our problems — ways in which we have, little by little, allowed untruths, with their accompanying powers to enslave and kill, to infect our nation. Finally, we will need to courageously reestablish time-tested principles of truth to promote healing of our nation as we go forward.

As we continue our pursuit of truth to set America free, it is essential we understand the nature of truth: God's principles of life will often contradict our natural instincts. That shouldn't come as a great surprise for those of us with a healthy appreciation for our own fallenness, our inherited sin nature that, among other things, impairs our ability to see with total clarity. It is because of this reality that we do need God's eternal perspectives on life. And his concepts are often startling, yet refreshingly wonderful as we allow them to penetrate our hearts and minds. Consider, for example, Jesus' Sermon on the Mount in which he challenges us with some pretty remarkable commands: *Turn the other cheek. Love your enemies. Don't worry. Lay up treasures in heaven. Give to the poor. Pray and fast in secret.*

Similarly, many of the Bible's instructions for establishing and running a civil society are not what common sense or our minds apart from God and his Word would always dictate. I'm talking about biblical principles such as:

- The intrinsic value of each human being, created in the image of God

- Man's tendency to sin and live for himself

- God's plan for marriage, sexuality, and family

- Ownership of private property

- God's plan for government

- God's exhortation for man to wisely yet

confidently utilize the resources God has placed
in this world

Many of those teachings, as well as others in the Bible,
are in direct conflict with the "wisdom" of current-day
societal "experts." And the experts have no lack of com-
pelling arguments to support their point of view. Truth
is subtle, and it often takes courage and faith to obey it,
sometimes blindly. Our framers and most Americans up
to our present day had this kind of courage and faith, and
our nation was much better for it. However, in our day, we
are tempted to reason everything with our minds apart
from God and, in our arrogance, run the risk of ignoring
God's plain teachings. We must still use our minds to reason things out, but humbly so, under the ultimate authority of Scripture. Wise King Solomon, in his earlier years,
put it well: *"There is a way that appears to be right, but in
the end it leads to death"* (Proverbs 14:12). He advises a
wiser course in Proverbs 3:5–6:

> *Trust in the LORD with all your heart*
> *and lean not on your own understanding;*
> *in all your ways submit to him,*
> *and he will make your paths straight.*

I want to see America set free again to soar as God and
our framers intended. I know that will require a coura-

geous look at where we are, a factual assessment of how we have gotten off track, and a plan to return to a place of safety and future health and growth.

I invite you to join me on a brief journey that will help us reclaim what we as a nation have lost. I

> I want to see America set free again to soar as God and our framers intended.

have intentionally kept this book short so that it can be easily read, absorbed, and passed on to others. My prayer is that this small book will spark revival of truth and its partner, grace, in our land, one person at a time — and that true healing will come, and come none too soon.

2

Government:
All or Nothing?

WE NEED TO UNDERSTAND SOME FUNDAMENTAL truths about God's view of government and what our role should be as citizens.

For starters, there is wide diversity of opinion among Christians as to where government fits in God's economy. At one extreme is Christian Reconstructionism, a small fringe movement founded by Rousas John Rushdoony, who taught that civil government should simply implement the Mosaic law's penal sanctions. Under such a system, the list of civil crimes that carry a death sentence would include homosexuality, adultery, incest, lying about one's virginity, bestiality, witchcraft, idolatry or apostasy, public blasphemy, false prophesying, kidnapping, rape, and bearing false witness in a capital case. I reject Christian Reconstructionism because I believe the reconstructionists misread Scripture. These laws were intended only for God's special nation of Israel — not for general application.

On the other extreme are people who teach that government is evil personified — that government, by definition, is under the control of Satan and therefore must be avoided by true followers of Christ.

> When I angrily threaten a legislator with negative repercussions if he doesn't vote my way —caring far more for his vote than his heart— I am *wrong*.

Most Christians fall somewhere between these widely divergent extremes. But few Christians I have met base their position on the subject on solid biblical exposition. Their view about how involved they should become in government and politics changes from day to day, depending on how busy they are in other areas of their lives and how angry they become about some court decision or law that threatens the comfort or safety of their families. As in most areas of life, healthy balance in politics is critical — though often difficult to maintain in practice. To help move us in the direction of balance, let me offer two clarifying assertions: First, *government is not all-important.* And second, *while not all-important, government is still essential, requiring significant involvement from sincere Christians.*

Government Is Not All-Important

Government is temporary; people are permanent.

During my time as executive director of Michigan Family Forum, I used to love to visit with legislators and others in government who disagreed with me on issues we felt were important to children and families in our state. God truly gave me a heart of love for these government figures. Sure, I wanted them to vote our way, and I did my best to convince them of the wisdom of our positions. But I saw clearly that underneath it all was not just a person who can vote on — or in some cases decide — an issue of public policy. Underneath was a person God dearly loves and with whom he longs to have a relationship. When I angrily threaten a legislator with negative repercussions if he doesn't vote my way — caring far more for his vote than his heart — I am *wrong.* There is a place in government for give and take, for giving (or withholding) something in exchange for something I want. But that give and take need never be conducted out of a heart of malice, bitterness, or rage.

I say this fully aware that I am touching a sensitive nerve among many politically active readers. You feel totally justified in your anger toward your representative, senator, governor, or president for actions or inactions that seem indefensible. After all, we're paying their salaries! They're supposed to be working for us, and they've done a poor job! If that describes your attitude, and you have a hard time transcending — or have no desire to transcend — anger toward governmental officials — hold this thought until chapter 5, where we'll discuss in more detail a biblical and godly way to interact with our leaders.

Good laws and good leaders do not guarantee a good nation.

There was a time when Israel had the best king ever, and the nation's laws were impeccable in terms of adhering to God's principles. Yet the nation was nonetheless under the judgment of Almighty God. I'm referring to the time when King Josiah ruled over the southern kingdom of Judah.

It was during Josiah's reign that the law of God, which had been long ignored, was found and read to the people. In 2 Kings 23:3, the king and all the people pledged to follow the law of God:

> The king stood by the pillar and renewed the covenant in the presence of the LORD — to follow the LORD and keep his commands, regulations and decrees with all his heart and all his soul, thus confirming the words of the covenant written in this book. Then all the people pledged themselves to the covenant.

Mind you, these people didn't just have the U.S. Constitution and our American legal system — they had a *perfect* set of laws given by God himself!

They also had the best king ever — apparently better even than King David:

> Neither before nor after Josiah was there a king like him who turned to the LORD as he did — with all his heart and with all his soul and with all his strength, in accordance with all the Law of Moses.
>
> (2 Kings 23:25)

Despite this governmental near-perfection, the nation was still headed for God's imminent judgment. Second

Kings 23:26 tells us that "the LORD did not turn away from the heat of his fierce anger."

Jeremiah 3 tells us why. Verse 6 informs us that the pronouncements recorded in this chapter were made during the reign of Josiah. In verse 10, we see that the commitment of the people to God was superficial at best: " 'Judah did not return to me with all her heart, but only in pretense,' declares the LORD."

The strength of a nation does not flow down from its government; it flows up from the character of its people. What shields a nation from the judgment of God is not good laws nor good leaders, as important as they are, but rather true righteousness in the heart of its people. "Righteousness exalts a nation, but sin is a disgrace to any people" (Proverbs 14:34). And true righteousness cannot come down from laws — not during the reign of Josiah in ancient Israel, and not now in the United States of America. Rather, it must emanate from the hearts and lives of the people. It must begin with you and me.

Human government will not exist forever.

Despite the attention our mass media gives to government and politics, both are temporary. Not only will they not exist in heaven, politicians don't have a very long shelf life down here either.

In 1990, Michigan State Senator John Engler was the Republican candidate for governor of Michigan. President George H. W. Bush campaigned on Engler's behalf, and my wife Marcia and I were invited to a reception at which Bush would be posing for photographs with supporters. When our turn came, the president

> The strength of a nation does not flow down from its government; it flows up from the character of its people.

took time to put one arm around Marcia and the other around me and force yet another smile for the camera. While I'm sure it was tedious for the president, it was great fun and very exciting for those of us who'd come to the reception specifically to meet him.

At the other end of the reception room, sitting largely by himself, was candidate Engler. At that time, no one gave the little-known Engler much chance of beating the multiterm incumbent Governor James Blanchard.

The election occurred a few weeks later. In a surprising upset, Engler narrowly beat Blanchard. A month or so later, Marcia and I attended one of Engler's statewide inaugural balls. While, just a few weeks before, Engler had been a lowly state senator, he was now governor-elect. I wanted to congratulate Engler at his inaugural ball, but I couldn't get within ten feet of him because of the press of the crowd.

Two years later, President Bush began his transition to Citizen Bush, a journey John Engler himself made twelve years later when he left the office of governor. While, now that they are just citizens, we still respect them, the glow and public adulation is gone.

So it is with politics and fame in general. If you dedicate your life solely to helping people get elected or influencing public policy, your earthly legacy will evaporate like the morning dew.

While Not All-Important, Government Is Still Essential

Human government is God's idea for mankind.

Because of our sin nature, we humans inevitably tend toward greediness and self-seeking. Government is God's idea to protect the innocent from those who would take advantage of them.

When we are wronged, our natural inclination is to get even. But in Romans 12, Paul tells us not to pay back evil for evil. In words consistent with Christ's exhortations in the Sermon on the Mount, Paul says that it's God's job to settle the score. In Romans 12:19, we specifically read, "Do not take revenge, my friends, but leave room for God's wrath, for it is written: 'It is mine to avenge; I will repay,' says the Lord." So the Bible clearly gives us two instructions we should follow when wronged: (1) Don't take revenge (in fact, on a personal level, we are to love; see Matthew 5:38–48), and (2) Leave room for God's wrath.

What does this have to do with government?

Government is God's earthly means of settling accounts and promoting justice. In the first few verses of Romans 13, we see Paul making this case. In fact, in 13:4, he refers to government as "God's servant." The Greek word *diakonos,* translated in English here as "servant," is elsewhere in the New Testament translated "deacon." Literally, government is God's "deacon boy" to do his bidding. And what is God's bidding? He wants government to be "an agent of wrath to bring punishment on the wrongdoer." So, in Romans 12:19 we are commanded to leave room for God's wrath, and in 13:4 we are told that government *is* the agent or means of God's wrath.

The Apostle Peter communicates the same thought in 1 Peter 2:13–14:

Submit yourselves for the Lord's sake to every authority instituted among men: whether to the king, as the supreme authority, or to governors, who are sent by him to punish those who do wrong and to commend those who do right.

When I was a prosecutor and later a judge, I was daily reminded — and humbled — by this reality. I saw myself as God's hands and feet to bring God's punishment on wrongdoers and protecting the innocent from those who would hurt them. It's not that I'm sinless and therefore qualified to personally stand in judgment over others. Not at all. But God is powerful enough to work through fallible men and women to promote a sense of justice in society.

It is exciting that God, in his sovereignty and power, is well able to use those in authority to do his bidding, whether they are conscious of it or not. In John 19:10–11, Jesus' interaction with Pilate the governor illustrates God's power as the "King of Kings":

"Do you refuse to speak to me?" Pilate asked. "Don't you realize I have power either to free you or to crucify you?"

Jesus answered, "You would have no power over me if it were not given to you from above."

Likewise, Emperor Caesar Augustus was used by God to have Jesus born in Bethlehem as had been prophesied centuries before (Luke 2:1–7). The wicked High Priest Caiaphas, who longed to kill Jesus, was nevertheless still used by God to speak amazing truth about Christ because of his leadership role (John 11:49–52).

Beyond its primary role promoting justice and order in society, government has other roles outlined or at least implied in Scripture. These will be discussed later in this book.

As a Christian citizen, you have a responsibility to government.

Government is ordained by God. But what does Scripture say about my obligation to government, as a citizen?

First, from Romans 13:1–6, I see I have the duty to respect this authority, to give it due honor, and to pay its taxes.

Beyond that is the biblical command to *pray* for those in civil authority.

> I urge, then, first of all, that requests, prayers, intercession and thanksgiving be made for everyone — for kings and all those in authority, that we may live peaceful and quiet lives in all godliness and holiness.
> (1 Timothy 2:1–2)

This command prompts a logical question: If we *don't* pray for those in authority, is it possible we will *not* live "peaceful and quiet lives in all godliness"? Put another way, do prayers for those in government actually work to bring us an environment in which we are able to live godly lives? I think, in fact, that is a fair and honest reading of this passage. If we value peace, quietness, and godliness, it's high time to renew our commitment to pray for our authorities.

The command to pray for those in authority is also found in the Old Testament. It's part of a letter written by the prophet Jeremiah to the Jewish exiles who were living at the time in Babylon, where they had been taken by their Babylonian captors. Apparently, false prophets were telling these captives that their time of exile would soon end, and they would be returning to Jerusalem. To counteract these lies, the prophet Jeremiah wrote, under God's inspiration, telling the Jewish exiles that the length of their captivity would be seventy years. He also added this command from God:

> This is what the LORD Almighty, the God of Israel, says to all those I carried into exile from Jerusalem to Babylon: "Build houses and settle down; plant gardens and eat what they produce. Marry and have

sons and daughters; find wives for your sons and give your daughters in marriage, so that they too may have sons and daughters. Increase in number there; do not decrease. *Also, seek the peace and prosperity of the city to which I have carried you into exile. Pray to the LORD for it, because if it prospers, you too will prosper."*

(Jeremiah 29:4–7, emphasis added)

Almighty God wanted his chosen people who lived in this foreign land to settle down, to make that place a home for themselves and their children. They were to "seek the peace and prosperity" of Babylon. Though Jeremiah provided few specifics on how to comply with this command, one method was clear: They were to pray for Babylon.

That's easy enough, we might think. But think again. Imagine that you are one of the Jewish exiles. Babylon was a fierce, cruel nation, one whose soldiers had probably ruthlessly raped, mistreated, and even killed many of your friends and family members. Their army had confiscated all your earthly possessions and burned your home to the ground. They had forced you to walk, half-naked and in chains, to Babylon. The Babylonians were pagans who did not worship or even acknowledge the one true

God. And now your God asks you to pray for Babylon's peace and prosperity. No way! If you pray about Babylon at all, it's going to be that God will judge and destroy it!

Why does God expect us to pray for the "peace and prosperity" of regimes we consider to be oppressive or immoral? Because he is able to work his will through even godless governments and leaders. Prayers for our nation will, ideally, cause even cruel despots to provide an environment of relative peace — quiet that allows us to pursue godliness. So if God can't motivate us to pray for our leaders out of the goodness of our hearts, perhaps we can be motivated by self-interest. Here in Jeremiah 29 we are told: "because if it [your nation] prospers, you too will prosper." Or, put the other way, if our nation doesn't prosper, neither will we.

> Why does God expect us to pray for the "peace and prosperity" of regimes we consider to be oppressive or immoral? Because He is able to work His will through even godless governments and leaders.

Like it or not, all of us in America today are riding this big ship of state. There are good people and bad, Christians, Muslims, Jews, agnostics, and atheists. Pastors, teachers, homemakers, doctors, lawyers, plumbers, farmers, as well as drug dealers, abortionists, and criminals. If our ship hits an iceberg, we're all going down to the icy depths. To the degree we value our lives and those of our children, we will heed the command to seek the peace and prosperity of our nation. As Benjamin Franklin put it, "We must all hang together or hang separately."

Ah, but you say, our nation is *so* godless and out of control. Our leaders seem intent on merely getting reelected and will promise anything to keep their positions of power. We read about insider trading and crony capitalism through which congressmen and senators fill their campaign coffers and sometimes line their own pockets. And our citizens seem intent on living lives that are an affront to a holy God. Consider legalized abortion, the push for same-sex marriage, hard-core pornography, our "hooking up" culture, high divorce rates, and much more. Granted. There are many, many problems — to the point that we can easily become discouraged. But it is still true that we need God's blessing on our nation for it to survive. We must not give up — rather, we must redouble our prayers for our nation and for our people to turn from sin to him. Resist the temptation to adopt the short-timer attitude: "Well, Jesus will be returning soon, so why worry about this mess?"

While we are commanded to be ready for Christ's

return, we also don't know when it will happen. It is not blasphemous to suggest that he may not return for five hundred more years. Just as God wanted the Jewish captives to settle down in Babylon, I believe he wants us to settle down in America, to build our homes and families and seek the peace and prosperity of the nation we have been placed in. I personally don't want to get to heaven and be asked why I spent so much time in front of the TV and so little time on my knees praying for the nation I was placed in — this nation that is the ship of state that will carry the ones I love into the future.

Besides prayer, how else can we seek the peace and prosperity of our nation? Some of you will be led by God to become actively involved in government at the local, state, or federal level. I certainly feel a call to do that. The prophet Daniel and his three friends helped rule Babylon. Esther was a Queen; Nehemiah worked for the king. But the vast majority of Jews were not part of the ruling class. The most they could do was to be honest, hard-working citizens who prayed regularly for their nation and its leaders, seeking its well-being. As Americans, even ordinary citizens have more ability to influence our government than the ancient Jews in Babylon had. This chapter will conclude with some practical ideas on how you can make a difference. But at the heart of all our actions as citizens must be our *attitudes*. Rather than cynicism or indifference, attitudes that control too many Christians today, we should have an appropriate loyalty toward our nation and proper respect of its leaders regardless of their political party.

Scripture says that God is sovereign in setting up leadership. We need to honor his choices with our prayers even if we find it challenging to honor the person in office.

Good public policy is really loving your neighbor.

Imagine that there's a dangerous intersection a mile or so from your home that seems to be a magnet for accidents. While it's a two-way stop in one direction, the cross street, which has no stop signs, winds around a corner and up a hill, making it difficult for those stopped to see oncoming traffic. In the last year alone, accidents at this intersection have killed three people and critically injured five.

As you discuss the matter with neighbors, you conclude that the county road commission should install a traffic light at this intersection. You decide to get neighbors to circulate a petition to get the commission's attention. After meeting with the officials, and after a study that seems to take far too long, a traffic signal is installed. Over the next years, the accident rate is much reduced, and fewer people are hurt or killed.

You just engaged in shaping public policy! The mere fact that it was local and didn't involve legislation doesn't detract from the fact that you took steps to influence government.

Was this action on your part somehow inappropriate entanglement with this world? Is there something in the Bible that mandates Christians to wait until the situation is dire before we can act? Are preventive measures the sole province of nonbelievers? The answer to these questions should be obvious.

The Good Samaritan in Jesus' parable came to the aid of a Jew beaten by robbers and left for dead. Certainly, we are encouraged to help with the tangible needs of those who have been hurt. But what if the Samaritan could have influenced the authorities to station a guard on the treacherous road to Jericho? Is it less loving to prevent injury than to help heal it? God doesn't frown on preventative steps: "When you build a new house, make a parapet around your roof so that you may not bring the guilt of bloodshed on your house if someone falls from the roof" (Deuteronomy 22:8).

Similarly, what if you have the leverage to impact the

sex education curriculum being taught in every high school in your state? What if you can make foundational to that curriculum the teaching that sex ideally belongs within the confines of a lifelong, monogamous, hetero-sexual marriage? And what if, because of that curriculum, thousands of kids in your state refrain from premarital sex? While this teaching may not have a direct spiritual impact on these young people, it is nonetheless loving to tell them the truth about life. We tell them, "Look both ways before you cross the street," and we all acknowledge that this is a wise precaution. Is it any less wise to provide solid moral guidance? This is another way to promote the peace and prosperity of your state.

All good public policy has as its ultimate goal the bet-terment of individuals and families. Admittedly, it isn't always easy to know with precision what will, in the long run, be best. On many issues, good people will come to differing conclusions. But that doesn't negate the need to get involved and seek God's wisdom on issues that clearly impact the lives of people God loves.

One of my heroes, William Wilberforce, was a member of parliament in nineteenth-century England. Motivated by his love for God and his fellow country-men, Wilberforce spent his lifetime pursuing two goals: (1) the elimination of the slave trade, and (2) the reform of "manners" (his term for a religious revival). It took incredible courage, much prayer, and dogged determination over many years to accomplish these goals. His book *Practical Christianity* is credited with helping to spark the Second Great Awakening, which revolutionized England and fanned the flames of revival in America as well. Clearly, Wilberforce was a Christian who was not afraid to get involved in national politics in a way that moved the nation closer to biblical values and that promoted the general peace and prosperity. We need to pray for many Wilberforces to rise in our day.

In America, where citizens are shareholders in our nation, Christians have a unique role.

Most citizens in ancient Babylon had little ability to influence public policy. The King's word was law. He had the total power of life and death over every citizen.

Similarly, in Jesus' and Paul's day, the Roman Emperor reigned supreme, delegating some of his civil power to the governors under him. The typical Roman citizen had little ability to influence decisions made by those in authority.

The United States of America was founded not by the elite and already powerful but by *us*:

We the people of the United States, in order to form a more perfect union, establish justice, insure domestic tranquility, provide for the common defense, promote the general welfare, and secure the blessings of liberty to ourselves and our posterity, do ordain and establish this Constitution for the United States of America.*

Abraham Lincoln captured this thought in his masterpiece of a speech at Gettysburg:

Fourscore and seven years ago our fathers brought forth on this continent a new nation, conceived in liberty and dedicated to the proposition that all men are created equal.... It is rather for us to be dedicated to the great task remaining before us ... that this nation, under God, shall have a new birth of freedom, and that *government of the people, by the people, for the people, shall not perish from the earth.*†

With the growth in size and complexity of government in recent years and the simultaneous growth of cynicism in our people, it's tempting to feel increasingly detached from what goes on in Washington, D.C., our state capitals, and even in our city halls. But we citizens

---

* Preamble to the U.S. Constitution, emphasis added.

† Gettysburg Address, Lincoln, November 19, 1863, emphasis added.

still ultimately own our government and have recourse when leaders attempt to exceed their lawful authority. So if we fail to do our part to correct these and other abuses in power, we will not escape culpability. "One who is slack in his work is brother to one who destroys" (Proverbs 18:9). If we have a job to do, and we have been given authority to do it, we need to act.

And what, in specific terms, is that job? What is the typical Christian citizen's obligations toward good governance? Chapter 5 will cover some of these action steps in greater detail, but here is, in my opinion, a good "laundry list" of privileges for the "shareholders" in American government. And I do consider these not just responsibilities but privileges — opportunities that were clearly not afforded those Jewish exiles in ancient Babylon, or the vast majority of citizens alive at the time of Christ, or, for that matter, most people in the world today outside the free world:

I believe we all need to:

1. Pray for our nation and leaders (including leaders in all three branches of government, legislative, executive, and judicial);

2. Be citizens of good moral character and integrity, and do our best to raise our children to become good citizens;

3. Register to vote (statistics I have seen suggest that only about half of eligible Christians are registered to vote);

4. Vote at every election we can;

5. Keep informed on issues of concern;

6. Communicate appropriately with our leaders about our feelings on issues that concern us;

7. Financially support good candidates for public office;

8. Be open to possible involvement in local party politics, and even consider running for local school boards, positions in county or city commissions, for state legislator, judge, or whatever else God may lead you to do.

3

Liberty: God's Gift or Man's Creation?

ONE OF MY FONDEST MEMORIES AT MICHIGAN FAMily Forum was the time I debated Howard Simon, head of the Michigan's chapter of the ACLU (American Civil Liberties Union).

Meeting at a packed union hall in Flint, Michigan, we were to spar on how best to preserve our civil liberties. While Howard is a real gentleman, I imagine that, as the time for the debate approached, he felt smug about his ability to make mincemeat of me — particularly among his ideological partners. As I drove to the meeting place, I earnestly prayed for help.

As the debate began, I could sense that the crowd

was almost gleeful in their anticipation of seeing this goody-two-shoes right-winger get his ears pinned back. But as I patiently communicated my thoughts about the actual source of our liberties and what it will take to preserve them, I sensed the crowd warming to me. I wasn't there to put down my opponent or to deride those who might disagree with me; I genuinely desired to share what I believed about the source of our liberties. In time, instead of derisive smirks, people were beginning to listen intently. Some even nodded in agreement. Before the debate was over, I even sensed my liberal opponent Howard Simon beginning to enjoy our interaction. At the end, he publicly acknowledged that he too believed in moral absolutes — not something an ACLU leader typically does. In all, I felt it was truly a blessed event.

Conventional wisdom says that the intolerance of those who hold to moral absolutes undermines the expansion of our civil rights — unlike the attitudes of more open-minded and tolerant citizens. As the argument goes, society advances as we discard the authoritarian rules of the past and discover new rights which liberate expanding categories of people — including children, women, gays, lesbians, and transgendered. If as Christians we challenge the propriety of expanding these rights on moral grounds, we are viewed as obstructionists to the natural progression of civilized humanity and called derisive names like homophobes. And woe to us if we even whisper the Bible's eternal perspectives on these cultural issues; that only reinforces our stereotype of being totally brainless and probably heartless.

Little wonder we Christians are unwelcome at the public policy table, since our involvement seems simpleminded at best and downright destructive at worst. With this sort of rejection, we find another good reason to relegate public policy to the non-believing world.

But my experience in Flint that day reminded me that the world desperately needs our perspectives — even if they don't realize it at first. If we love our neighbor, we need to speak the truth in love.

> The world desperately needs our perspectives — even if they don't realize it at first. If we love our neighbor, we need to speak the truth in love.

And the truth I shared in my debate that day is that everybody — Christian, agnostic, atheist, conservative, liberal, and everyone in between — loves liberty. We all love being able to live, work, play, speak, write, and worship as we please. No one group is more attached to liberty than any other. The human soul loves freedom to be what he or she has been created to be. We love this about our country.

Beyond that, virtually everyone also agrees that human liberty needs boundaries. Reasonable limits must be established to limit our freedom lest the resulting anarchy harm people and property.

But how do you decide *where* to draw the lines, where to establish laws that limit our freedom? What should these laws be? Which actions should we allow, and which actions should we declare to be crimes?

The answers to these questions provide the foundation for our entire system of laws — laws that impact us all.

Placing Limits on Our Liberties

In deciding how limits should be placed on human liberty, there are two and *only* two options:

1. We humans decide *for ourselves, apart from God,* how far our liberty should go and what its limits should be.

2. We humans look to the Creator God and his commandments spelled out in Scripture to establish limits to our liberty.

Throughout history, there have been champions for each of these approaches. Most people today have adopted one position or the other without much thought. But as we stated in the first chapter, if our choices in life are based on truth, we will promote genuine liberty. And if our life choices are built on lies — even if they appear to be truthful — we will inadvertently promote bondage. Let's look at these two competing views and analyze which is truthful and which is not.

APPROACH #1: We humans decide for ourselves, apart from God, how far our liberty should go and what its limits should be.

It might help to envision this first approach this way:

I've used dashed lines to represent the limits on our liberty to indicate that they aren't permanent, but rather flexible and moveable. If we as people want to expand our rights, we can do so through legislation, regulation, or judicial decree. For example, if we decide one day to allow ourselves greater access to materials previously outlawed as pornographic, we can do so.

The same flexibility could be applied to the right of women to seek an abortion, the right to apply for a job without being asked about our marital status or sexual orientation, the right to be in an airplane without tobacco products being used by others, the right to carry a handgun, and so on.

As we decide which laws to enact to place limits on our liberties, we don't consult any outside source to tell us what is *right* or *wrong*. We may look at scientific evidence, such as studies on the harm caused by secondhand smoke; we may study polling data to understand what people want or don't want. But we don't base our choice on any ultimate sense of what is immutably right or wrong from God's point of view.

By insisting on the ability to modify our laws virtually at the will of the majority, we as a people are well-positioned to change with evolving standards of morality for many generations to come.

APPROACH #2: We humans look to the Creator God and his commandments spelled out in Scripture to establish limits to our liberty.

In contrast to Approach #1 where we simply decide as people what we feel will best meet our needs at the moment, in Approach #2, we sense an obligation to discern God's view of human liberty, of conduct that is right or wrong.

On its face, this approach seems anachronistic and inflexible and therefore greatly inferior to Approach #1. To modern minds, it might seem that those supporting this approach must be living in nostalgia for bygone times. But let's look more closely.

To show Approach #2 graphically, I depict it with solid lines circumscribing our liberty:

Solid lines suggest that liberty's limits are fixed because they are imprinted on the moral fabric of the universe by its Creator, almighty God. Ideally, those of us who believe in Approach #2 and who believe that the universe was created by God also believe that he created it with clear intentions — and we want our laws to be in harmony with those intentions. We want to go *with* the "grain" of the universe, not against it. For example, why do we determine that murder is outside the limits of our liberty? Not primarily because we decide, as humans, that this is a wise policy, but rather because the Creator and Sustainer of the universe says, "Thou shalt not kill" — murder is wrong for all time and for all cultures. Any attempt to tamper with this prohibition goes against an authority much larger than man himself. So, from this perspective, euthanasia ("mercy" killing) and infanticide (killing of unwanted newborns) — both advocated by various groups today — would be wrong.

Which Approach Is Best?

There are certain behaviors — like murder, or sexual exploitation of children, or theft, or assault — that nearly everyone would agree should be outside the realm of accepted liberties, and that's why nearly all societies, all countries, have laws against them. Other behaviors, though, such as drug usage, aberrant sexual behaviors, abortion, and pornography, are reviled by some but defended by others. And to call such behaviors absolutely wrong rankles cultural elites and flies in the face of conventional wisdom. It's so old-fashioned and backwater — like living your life based on old wives' tales and urban legends.

But the catch is this: when you replace rigid lines limiting our liberty with dashed ones, you also make our liberties themselves fragile and subject to removal when societal values change. The lines — whether dashed or solid — establish not only the *limits* to our liberty but also the existence of our liberty itself. If the lines collapse, our liberty vanishes as well. In other words, if the lines are flexible, permitting us more liberty at one point in time, they can also flex in the other direction and take it away at another time.

The signers of our Declaration of Independence understood this well. They saw that we need God not only to prescribe the limits to our liberty, but to give us our precious liberty in the first place:

> We hold these truths to be self-evident, that all men are created equal, that they are endowed *by their Creator* with certain unalienable Rights, that among these are Life, Liberty and the pursuit of Happiness. That to secure these rights, Governments are

instituted among Men, deriving their just powers from the consent of the governed.*

Rights, taught our framers, are gifts from our Creator. Governments don't give rights — rather, they were designed to *preserve* these God-given rights. The framers understood that, if God gives us rights, no human — whether an individual or a group of people — has the legitimate authority to take these rights away. However, if the lines protecting our liberty are flexible, if man expands them based on his own whims, he can legitimately shrink them as well.

> The framers understood that, if God gives us rights, no human — whether an individual or a group of people — has the legitimate authority to take these rights away.

For society to function, individual rights will always be subject in some ways to limitation to preserve the good of society as a whole and to protect the rights of other individuals. In reality, when you protect the rights of certain individuals or groups, you often at the same time restrict the rights of others. For example, when you expand the right of potential

---

* *Declaration of Independence*, emphasis added.

employees not to be asked certain questions in their job interviews, you simultaneously reduce the ability of an employer to make the best fit between the candidate and his business. When government accedes to the request of the green lobby to protect a plant species in a wetland area, the landowner's use of his "private" property is impaired. When, for the sake of women's interests, you expand the right of pregnant females to "terminate" their pregnancies, you literally (and legally) snuff out the lives of millions of unborn boys and girls.

In 1989, the passion for freedom pushed its way into communist mainland China. Thousands of citizens staged peaceful protests for liberty and against totalitarian rule in Beijing's Tiananmen Square. Their dream was for China to follow the lead of so many Eastern European communist nations at that time as they moved toward self-rule. In a touching scene on TV, Chinese young people stood with resolve next to miniature replicas of our Statue of Liberty. They quoted the stirring prose of our Declaration of Independence.

And then the tanks rolled in. The Chinese protesters were forcibly removed and official order restored. Many of us — perhaps you? — believed at the time that the Chinese government was wrong. But if man is the author of his own liberty, he can rightly choose to take it away at will. When men claim the right to make the rules without any reference to an external moral standard, they become a god unto themselves. Might makes right.

In my debate with ACLU's Howard Simon, I suggested to the crowd that I like my liberty to be "industrial strength," and that, in fact, it is — because it was given to us by our Creator, and not by any human source. As I said this, both the crowd and Howard himself seemed to move in my direction. After all, who doesn't want their rights to be secure from tampering? Thomas Jefferson, though, was afraid of that very thing — that we might lose them altogether. Engraved on the walls of the Jefferson Memorial in Washington are his words:

> When men claim the right to make the rules without any reference to an external moral standard, they become a god unto themselves.

> God who gave us life gave us liberty. Can the liberties of a nation be secure when we have removed a conviction that these liberties are the gift of God?*

If that's not reason enough to choose Approach #2, I

---

* From Panel 3 of the Jefferson Memorial, Washington, D.C.

can suggest two other reasons why this approach is superior to Approach #1: (1) it promotes America as a "melting pot" rather than a "salad bowl"; and (2) it fosters true self-government.

Promoting America as a melting pot rather than a salad bowl

If our rights are decided by the whim of man, then man also gets to decide what is right and what is wrong, what is criminal and what is legal, without any regard to what God has to say on the issue. We could make it illegal to eat peanut-butter-and-jelly sandwiches or to smile in public. We could make it legal to steal from your neighbor or to assault someone simply because he disagrees with you.

We may laugh at these examples. But the laughter stops when we look at man-made laws that have been imposed upon us with no apparent regard to God's law. For example, On January 22, 1973, the U.S. Supreme Court in the case of *Roe v Wade* ruled that no longer could a state criminalize abortion, the killing of a child *in utero*. The Court ruled that the due process clause of the Fourteenth Amendment requires this finding. The due process clause, passed in 1868 for reasons that had nothing to do with abortion, reads as follows: "nor shall any state deprive any person of life, liberty or property without due process of law." A majority of our Supreme Court ruled that this means a woman has the right to "terminate her pregnancy" irrespective of the rights of the unborn, virtually throughout her pregnancy.

While this decision defied logic even in the eyes of many pro-abortion legal scholars, its specific impact on my state of Michigan took *illogic* to a new level. You see, on January 21, 1973, abortion was a felony crime that legitimately could be prosecuted in our state. But on January 22, this felony crime suddenly became a revered U.S. constitutional right! So now, along with the freedom of religion and the freedoms of speech and of the press — all guaranteed by the Bill of Rights — we have the freedom to take the life of a child God is forming in the womb. Our court changed what was formerly wrong to what was legal and therefore "right."

Changing rights also changes obligations. When a culture is free to decide right and wrong without any regard to external moral codes, it is highly likely that people will have widely differing definitions of what is right and wrong. And no one member or group in society can authoritatively say that any other person or group is incorrect: Everybody is entitled to his or her own opinion. Like the people in the time of the Judges in the Old Testament, "In those days there was no king in Israel. Everyone did what was right in his own eyes" (Judges 17:6, ESV).

The problem with this approach is that we would lose our identity as "one nation under God, indivisible, with liberty and justice for all." Nations, like cohesive families, are delicately held together by the *ideas* the citizens share in common. But when we lose this in our country, America becomes the home for many sub-nations, each with its own sense of identity, competing with the other sub-nations for legislation consistent with its view of right and wrong. No longer is America a melting pot with one common theme emanating from our founding documents and our Judeo-Christian worldview. We are a house divided.

Has America *ever* had total unanimity in its worldview? No. But even when a number of our early citizens were atheistic or agnostic, they at least understood that our American system was derived from a Judeo-Christian heritage, and were willing to live here with that knowledge. When in Rome, you do what the Romans do — and when in America, you do as Americans do. A nation need not apologize for its heritage, particularly when that heritage, while far from perfect, extends proper respect for the rights of others to practice their religions or non-religions. We will talk more about this in chapter 7.

Fostering self-government

As we Americans embrace the belief that our rights and moral obligations come from a God who lovingly weighs our words, actions, and motives, we will develop a conscience. We will do right because we want to please God, not just to avoid punishment or because we have decided, pragmatically, that it is wise to obey the law. This self-policing by our citizens is called *self-government*.

Our framers realized that our nation would not work well without self-government. You can't allow people to be free unless they are willing to monitor and control themselves. To the degree that people in our nation are unwilling to do this, the nation will need an ever-expanding bureaucracy to maintain order.

In the words of Edmund Burke in 1791:

> Men are qualified for civil liberty in exact proportion to their disposition to put moral chains on their own appetites.... Society cannot exist unless a controlling power upon will and appetite be placed somewhere, and the less of it there is within, the more there must be without. It is ordained in the eternal constitution of things, that men of intemperate minds cannot be free. Their passions forge their fetters.*

---

* From "A Letter to a Member of the National Assembly," 1791.

In his farewell address, George Washington provided wise counsel for our nation that we would do well to heed today:

> Of all the dispositions and habits which lead to political prosperity, religion and morality are indispensable supports. In vain would that man claim the tribute of patriotism who should labor to subvert these great pillars of human happiness — these firmest props of the duties of men and citizens. The mere politician, equally with the pious man, ought to respect and to cherish them.... Let it simply be asked, Where is the security for property, for reputation, for life, if the sense of religious obligation desert the oaths which are the instruments of investigation in courts of justice? And let us with caution indulge the supposition that morality can be maintained without religion.... [R]eason and experience both forbid us to expect that national morality can prevail in exclusion of religious principle.*

John Adams said, "Our Constitution was made for a moral and religious people. It is wholly inadequate to the government of any other."†

---

*Washington's Farewell Address, 1796.

†Letter to the Officers of the First Brigade of the Third Division of the Militia of Massachusetts, 11 October 1798.

You don't read much about "separation of church and state" in these comments. But how else can you allow 310 million people to be free unless the vast majority of us is willing to police ourselves according to some external standard? This self-policing or self-government is the key foundation for our nation's success. So many of the problems in other parts of the world arise from the *lack* of self-government in the lives of those nations' citizens.

If we in America feel we can make up our own rules of right and wrong, then each of us will have our own subjective and personal standard of good and evil. In such a situation, no one can legitimately impose his moral code on others: all codes are equally valid and invalid. But because we need some authority to prevent anarchy, government plays the role of the bully with the biggest stick, enforcing its version of morality. There's a built-in drawback with that model: If you can break the law without getting caught, consider yourself lucky, an example to be admired and emulated. Lawbreaking can occur without guilt or remorse. Your moral code, after all, is as valid as anyone else's — and as valid as the government's.

If, on the other hand, there is an objective, immutable standard of right and wrong, and a nation tries its utmost to reflect this standard in its laws, the government that enforces these laws is on the side of truth. People will then strive to obey the law for two reasons: (1) fear of legitimate punishment, and (2) for conscience's sake.

Having said this, an obvious practical question remains: How do we decide, specifically, what is the "objective, immutable standard of right and wrong?"

The English common law, which our Founders adopted *in toto*, came from the laws of King Alfred of tenth-century England. Alfred's laws began with the Ten Commandments and the laws of Moses, along with the Golden Rule given by Jesus.*

Sir William Blackstone of eighteenth-century England likewise felt that the Bible was the fundamental law undergirding our legal system:

> Upon these two foundations, the law of nature and the law of revelation, depend all human laws; that is to say, no human laws should be suffered to contradict these.†

Does that mean that we are limited to passing only laws that mirror God's laws? No. Blackstone discussed this as well in his *Commentaries*. It is proper for a government to limit our freedom in ways other than can be

---

* Harold J. Berman, *Law and Revolution: The Formation of the Western Legal Tradition* (Cambridge: Harvard University Press, 1983), 65.

† William Blackstone, *Commentaries on the Laws of England*, Vol. 1, 1735.

found in Scripture. Take, for example, motor vehicle laws, postal and tax regulations, licensing laws, etc. But the more governments proliferate laws totally unrelated to underlying principles of right and wrong, the more they run the risk of illegitimately restricting our liberty.

Even with these guidelines, it is not always easy to decide what laws to enact. But there is a world of difference between lawmakers who sincerely try their utmost to discern eternal concepts of right and wrong in their legislation and other lawmakers who simply pass legislation to please their constituents. Mistakes will be made in the best of worlds. And, when new light on a subject becomes available, laws can be changed.

For example, laws outlawing abortion were initially passed around the time of the Civil War with the goal of protecting a "quickened fetus." It was thought then that the unborn was not really alive until the mother could feel movement. We now know that a unique life begins at conception, and heartbeats and movement occur weeks before the mother can sense them. Laws against abortion have always been based on the sixth commandment's prohibition of murder — unlawfully taking the life of another person. It is imminently sensible that as we discover new evidence of how we humans are formed in the womb, these laws should be amended to protect unborn human babies from conception. That may well require a Human Life Amendment to the U.S. Constitution, unless our Supreme Court has the courage and wisdom to reverse *Roe v Wade*.

In this chapter, we've considered two vastly different approaches to establishing a system of laws. The first approach promises freedom, but results in less self-control, more confusion about right and wrong, and the need for an expanding and expensive central government to preserve order and to promulgate by fiat the ever-changing truth of the week. The second approach seems on the surface to be a poor choice because it requires both humility and much effort on our part — humility to admit we don't have all the answers, and effort when we struggle at times to discern how best to apply God's eternal perspectives to the complexities of our human existence. But applying truth to the discussion of the limits to our liberty is ultimately very liberating — it's like knowing where your neighbor's mailbox is when you back out of the driveway. By revealing the true guidelines of life and illuminating the consequences of bad decisions, truth enables us to avoid life's pitfalls.

4

Civil Society That Works

IN CHAPTER 2, WE TALKED ABOUT THE ROLES OF THE government and the citizen. I don't want to imply that those are the only two essential parts of society. God has also ordained that the "mediating institutions" of the church and the family also play a crucial role, particularly in a free society, for our nation to operate well. It is essential that each entity perform its unique function properly, and that each respect the autonomy of the others.

What are the minimally essential roles for each of these God-ordained institutions?

Government

The U.S. Constitution spells out the roles of our federal government. Each state's constitution does the same for the states. Here's an admittedly simplified list (for reasons of clarity and emphasis), based on constitutional directives, of what I consider to be the primary roles of our federal government:

1. *Defense:* To defend our nation from foreign enemies.

2. *Immigration:* To control our borders and establish a system of legal immigration.

3. *Criminal Justice:* To protect us from criminality; to apprehend, try in a court of law, and justly punish those who have been convicted of crime with the by-product of deterring potential offenders from breaking the law.

4. *Money:* To coin money and take steps to ensure the value of our money.

5. *Taxation:* To establish a fair and equitable system of taxation.

6. *Economy:* To pay our nation's bills.

7. *Fundamentals:* To preserve our God-given rights. This is spelled out in the Declaration of

Independence: "To secure these [God-given] rights, governments are instituted among men, deriving their just powers from the consent of the governed."

Church

In this chapter, I use the term "church" to describe faith institutions in general. I unapologetically am a follower of Christ, but I respect those in other religious traditions; in fact, Jesus commanded me to love all men as I love myself. While overwhelmingly Christian in its history, America has guaranteed and given more freedom of religion than any other nation in the history of the world. I want this to continue. Having said that, I will speak primarily here to those of a Christian perspective, and encourage our fellow citizens of a different religious persuasion to adapt my words to their teachings.

The three primary roles of the church are:

1. *Promoter of Godly Character:* To train and encourage church members to be true followers of Christ, toward the end that they will exhibit godly character at home, at work, and in the community.

2. *Source of Truth:* To proclaim the truth about

God's principles of life to individuals, families, and government.

3. **Source of Grace:** To help meet the needs of the poor and disadvantaged. Both Old and New Testaments speak of the need for God's people to care for the poor.

Family

The three primary roles of the family are:

1. **Source of Human Productivity:** To encourage each adult family member to discern and pursue his or her calling, whether at home or elsewhere, with diligence, perseverance, and godliness.

2. **Source of Human Capital:** To produce children, if God should so bless, and raise them to be people of good character desirous of pursuing their own calling with integrity and diligence.

3. **Source of Financial Capital:** To use the money earned by the family, contributing some to support the government in the form of taxes, some to the church in a tithe, and some to help the needs of the poor, particularly extended family members in need.

* * *

If these roles are critical for our civil society to function properly, it is fair to ask how we are doing. Let's start with the role of families: Are the adults in American homes really pursuing their callings with diligence? Are the parents raising children of good character?

How about the churches: Are our churches consistently making disciples? Are they courageously communicating truth that informs and enables government to promote maximum liberty and life in our nation? Are churches helping to meet the needs of the poor?

For our federal government: Is Washington protecting our God-given rights to life, liberty, and the pursuit of happiness? Does our criminal justice system really deter much crime and produce justice? Is our tax code fair, equitable, and easy to understand? Is government making our money supply strong? Are we paying our bills?

It's painful to ask these questions, because the answers are almost all negative. Little wonder our nation is languishing.

And we need to ask more than whether the government, the church, and the family are doing their role. We must also consider whether they have usurped roles that God has designed for another institution and not them.

For example, what if government, with the best of intentions, declares war on poverty and takes over the role churches (and families, along with parachurch charities) should be doing? Or what if government, sensing that parents are doing an inadequate job raising children, decides to require its public schools to assume a parental role in teaching values and ethics — even though devoid of and detached from any moral or religious base?

When this kind of encroachment into the turf of another institution occurs, even though we may applaud the motivation to help, I can assure you that much more harm than good will actually result. A good example of that is the growth of the welfare state in America, which I will discuss in more detail in chapter 6. As I will explain, that misguided effort has inadvertently produced a great deal of human misery and economic disaster. Federal means-tested welfare programs have devastated our federal budget, made people perpetually dependent on government handouts, and broken up families. Genuine assistance to the poor takes much more than merely writing a check. It takes human-to-human contact to encourage,

> Government is simply not good at "leading or driving" the poor out of their poverty.

exhort, and sometimes walk away until the individual helps himself.

In 1766, Benjamin Franklin wrote in his article, "On the Price of Corn and the Management of the Poor," for the *London Chronicle*:

> I am for doing good to the poor, but I differ in opinion of the means. I think the best way of doing good to the poor, is not making them easy in poverty, but leading or driving them out of it. In my youth I travelled much, and I observed in different countries, that the more public provisions were made for the poor, the less they provided for themselves, and of course became poorer. And, on the contrary, the less was done for them, the more they did for themselves, and became richer.

Government is simply not good at "leading or driving" the poor out of their poverty.

How about when government attempts to perform the job that rightfully belongs to parents?

In recent years, public schools have become an arm of government and have assumed many roles formerly the exclusive province of the family. While the state has a clear interest in an educated citizenry, the education of children is ultimately the responsibility of parents.

In reaction to school programs that contradict families' values and in the hope of obtaining a higher-quality education for their children, many parents are now teaching their children at home. Other parents have banded together to form home-school clubs or have created private schools under the parents' control. The results of most of these parent-initiated programs have been positive.*

Originally, public schools were merely an extension of the home for the purpose of educating children in a given community. But we now have in place massive federal, state, and local bureaucracies to oversee education for children. This added bureaucracy has not resulted in better education. In fact, compared to other developed nations in the world, American public schools are deplorable. Listen to the findings of the Broad Foundation:

We are losing a generation of American minds. American students are not learning the skills and knowledge they need to succeed in today's world. Today, 70 percent of our eighth graders can't read proficiently and most of them will never catch up. Some 1.1 million American high school students drop out every year.

---

* For example, see research done by the Home School Legal Defense Fund at http://www.hslda.org/docs/nche/000010/200410250.asp.

Compared to the rest of the world, the state of education in America is disappointing and embarrassing. After World War II, the United States had the number 1 high school graduation rate. Today, we have dropped to number 21 among industrialized nations. American students rank 25th in math and 21st in science compared to students in 30 industrialized countries. Even America's top math students rank 25th out of 30 when compared with the best students across the globe. While America spends more money each year on education, we are losing more and more American students. While we agree that no American student should be left out, written off, or ignored, far too many of our poorest and minority students today still lack adequate resources to learn.[*]

Schools can and should do a much better job of educating children than they do. If parents without an education degree and without state teacher certification who homeschool their children can statistically out-perform the results from public schools, we should demand much more from our schools.

Teaching children to read is not rocket science.

---

[*] See http://www.broadeducation.org/about/crisis.html; see also http://www.cfr.org/united-states/us-education-reform-national-security/p27618.

Volumes of research performed over half a century consistently demonstrate that children from all socioeconomic backgrounds can successfully be taught to read. One can only guess why our education elites, who pride themselves in teaching and learning, fail to learn from this overwhelming evidence.

The fault does not primarily lie with classroom teachers. Teachers are a product of their education, and I know of no school of higher learning today that is doing an outstanding job of preparing teachers to teach Johnny to read.

I initially became sensitized to this issue years ago when my older children began the process of learning to read. Our kids were enrolled in what were considered to be exceptional suburban public and private schools. When our oldest child, Michelle, reached the right age to learn to read, Marcia and I kept waiting for Michelle's teacher to teach the sounds of letters and combinations of letters. Instead, Michelle was given a succession of little books to read without a modicum of instruction as to how to decipher the words. Sensing a problem, we started to teach phonics at home, hoping we weren't interfering with what the teacher was doing in class.

I'm so glad we did what we did! Michelle and our other children have learned to read well despite inadequate preparation in the classroom. And the sad reality is that data shows if kids don't learn to read reasonably well by age nine, they are destined to a lifetime of reading impairment. Considering the necessity of being able to read — increased ability to learn other subjects, plus the ability to read for enjoyment, not to mention the ability to read the Bible — we are significantly harming children if we deprive them this skill.

While the pendulum has swung back and forth over time, a substantial number of modern education theorists continue to adhere to a single view: They feel kids will learn to read "when they are ready."* In an extreme modern approach to teaching, the student becomes responsible for his own learning (it is said he "constructs" knowledge by interacting with his environment), leaving the teachers in the more passive role of facilitators, exonerating them from responsibility for the educational outcome. Therefore, to teach reading, this essentially means we surround the students with words and books. Children are taught to memorize a few words and try to learn new words not by "sounding out" phonetically but from the context — the pictures, the adjacent words, and so on.

During my tenure at Michigan Family Forum, I had

---

* See, for example, http://www.psychologytoday.com/blog/freedom-learn/201002/children-teach-themselves-read.

the privilege of making repeated visits to a school that seemed too good to be true. Mabel B. Wesley Elementary School is an inner-city, public elementary school in Houston, Texas. With 99 percent of the 1000 students in this school minority and most of them from single-parent families, you might assume, wrongly, that this school would provide a very substandard education. The reason for the school's success was its leadership. The principal of this school at the time of my visits was Thaddeus Lott, a burly and very gutsy black man with strong opinions and a deep love of children. Upon his arrival at Wesley in 1975, Lott fearlessly reorganized it in ways that flew in the face of popular but unsuccessful approaches to education.

The biggest change made by Lott was to retrain his teachers to actually *teach* their students, rather than merely "facilitate" the children's education. The teachers and students at Wesley work hard; throughout a typical school day, teachers and students are interacting, drilling, and memorizing with much verbal energy until the skills being taught are mastered. The results have been astounding.

Accompanying me on my trips to Wesley were a succession of education leaders from Michigan, including most of the members of the State Board of Education, some state legislators, and the head of our State Chamber of Commerce. At the school's invitation, we entered the classrooms to observe the kids. A favorite destination for me was the kindergarten classes — where I saw virtually every one of these five- and six-year-old students reading proficiently at the second-grade level, doing math at the same rate, and being able to tell me the name and location of every state in the U.S. from a map that showed only the outlines of states! By the time the Wesley students reach the fourth grade, they are reading and discussing Shakespeare's plays, while they continue to perform in math and other subjects at an advanced level.

Before 1975, when Thaddeus became principal of Wesley, only 18 percent of its third-graders were scoring at or above grade level in reading comprehension on the Iowa Test of Basic Skills. By 1980, 85 percent were achieving at or above grade level. In 1996, *100 percent* of Wesley's third-graders passed the Texas Assessment of Academic Skills (TAAS) in reading.

A small number of schools in other parts of the country have attempted to model the program at Wesley. I visited Arlington Park Elementary School in inner-city Columbus, Ohio, which employs a program patterned after Lott's successful approach in Houston. Arlington Park likewise experienced impressive, almost immediate gains in student reading and math levels when they made the changes. The year before principal Linda Gibson-Tyson implemented the changes, her school ranked near the bottom — 89th out of 93 Columbus-area elementary schools — in performance. In one year, they climbed to 27th out of 93, a rise so precipitous that the school district suspected cheating on standardized tests! However, an investigation by the city's education bureaucrats proved that the performance gain was real. What a difference the concerted efforts of a loving and courageous principal and her dedicated, flexible staff produced!

Isn't it strange that we don't make the same assumptions about learning nonacademic skills, such as sports or playing musical instruments, that modern educators do about teaching academic subjects? In these endeavors, we practice, practice, practice until the child develops mastery and, with it, a growth in self-esteem and confidence. But, inside the classroom, our education elites seem adverse to the notion that learning is hard, though very valuable, work. They even derisively mock the concept of repeated practice by touting the slogan "drill and kill." However, by *not* drilling, what's actually being killed is the future of America's children, especially those in most inner-city public schools.

The reality is that learning to read requires learning

the skill of decoding the sounds of words. Multiplication requires arduous memory of the multiplication table. Just as practicing your scales on the piano is not always thrilling, neither is the process of learning to read or do math. But once learned, these skills pay great dividends — especially learning to read.

Ideas have consequences. As we have been saying throughout this book, lies have power just as truth has power. To assume, wrongly, that Johnny will somehow learn to read, spell, add, subtract, multiply, and divide on his own, at his own pace and schedule, is a tragic myth that is hurting millions of American children. Teachers: quit passing your students on to the next grade in the hope that they will learn when they are ready to do so. Take the trouble and responsibility to teach them now! Parents, insist on this.

As the authority for educational policy over time has moved from parents to local school boards to state and federal governments, parents increasingly are feeling detached from their children's education. Not only have schools been failing academically, they are also devoting valuable classroom time to teaching students information that often contradicts families' views of American exceptionalism, sex, and morality in general.

Much of the driving force behind this movement are

society's social engineers who, in their quest for building a perfect society, feel parents are inadvertently slowing progress toward this goal when they impose, by word and example, their backwater religious, moral, and patriotic notions on their impressionable children.

It helps to remember who owns our children. Children do not belong to the state, but neither do we as parents own our children. Children are made by God (Psalms 127; 139), and, therefore, *he* owns them. Parents hold children in trust for God and are responsible to God to raise them in the "training and instruction of the Lord" (Ephesians 6:4). Parents, do not delegate your parental responsibility of raising your children to their schools — even to good parochial schools. The same goes for passing the baton to youth pastors, Christian camps, or seminars. All these resources can be helpful, but when you stand before the judgment seat of Christ, he will ask you what *you* did to train your child to follow him. Do your job with much prayer, example, humility that asks forgiveness when you blow it, and courage.

* * *

I can imagine many of those in education and other helping professions, after reading what I've written in this chapter, complaining that there are many parents who have indeed abdicated their responsibility in raising their children. I was a juvenile court judge for fifteen years and, believe me, I understand what you are saying. The problem of indifferent parenting is compounded by the staggering and tragic growth of the number of children born out of wedlock. Millions of American children are being raised without a dad. The sad truth is: Parents cannot be replaced by school counselors, any more than dads can be replaced by a welfare check.

When churches or parents drop the ball, the ball stays dropped — the schools cannot effectively put it back in play, no matter how hard they may try or how good their intentions.

There *is* a role for government in the rare instance when parents have caused actual neglect or abuse. But let me sprinkle a huge dose of reality here, speaking from years of experience as a judge, seeing tens of thousands of families: Government involvement is no guarantee that the situation will improve for any set of kids. With swollen caseloads and mere mortals as caseworkers, foster

> When churches or parents drop the ball, the ball stays dropped — the schools cannot effectively put it back in play, no matter how hard they may try or how good their intentions.

parents, and judges, there are all too many instances in which parental neglect is merely replaced by governmental ineptitude. Kids who have been hurt by their parents often languish in a succession of foster homes. When parents fail, government is a less than ideal but sometimes very necessary backup.

Our nation is not working well — because its parts are not working well. It's tempting — but unfair and dangerous — to place all the blame on government for our nation's problems. And it's true that government, especially our federal government, is not meeting its responsibilities very well at present. In fact, I'd have to give the federal government a very low grade. But many of our churches and many of our fragile American families are also not doing well at fulfilling their responsibilities to their members and to the nation and its people.

But rather than pointing the finger at others who are not stepping up to the plate, I need to start with me. Am I being the best follower of Christ, the best husband, father, grandfather, citizen, neighbor, employee, church member I can be? If not, why not? Who can I mentor to help along the way? Who can help hold me accountable? As a parent, how can I make sure my children are growing in Christ? Academically, are my children actually developing mastery of basic skills? If my children are attending school, what are they being taught about our governmental system, capitalism, the place of God in the forming of our nation, sexuality, morality, how the universe was fashioned and how life began?

If you believe, as I do, that our institutions and those in power, including school officials, need to improve the job they're doing on our behalf, pay close attention to the following chapter, in which we will talk about how to effectively influence people in authority.

5

Christian Citizenship 101

In the previous chapter, we discussed the responsibilities of government, the church, and the family in keeping our nation running well and moving in the right direction. We also concluded that none of the three is doing that job well! What happens when we followers of Christ believe that our voice needs to be heard in influencing government to do its job better? I'd like to suggest an approach that will enable us to impact our leaders in ways that reflect Christ and are, at the same time, effective.

My wife, Marcia, and I have been blessed with twelve children. Yes, this is a first marriage for both of us, and no, we have no twins or triplets and no adoptions: Marcia had them the hard way, one at a time. Our youngest is now an adult, and we are empty-nesters for the first time in forty years of child-rearing.

Has life with a dozen children been easy? No. We all know that life itself isn't easy, but God's call is truly God's enablement. He has marvelously met our needs in amazing ways.

Many parents would agree that one of parentings' greatest challenges arises from certain children who are "strong-willed." We have had a few of these unique children in our mix. My working definition of a strong-willed child is one who feels called to run your family. Yes, this is a challenge — and a surprise to parents who are not themselves strong-willed. But I have grown to love strong-willed kids, because in my mind they are, by nature, leaders who have simply taken their role too far and need to be dialed back.

While by no means the first or only one of our children possessing a strong will, our youngest child, Nathan, certainly falls into this category. As he grew up, Nathan had to learn — often the hard way, with discipline — how to control his tendency to run our household. There were plenty of times when Nathan would angrily challenge my authority on some decision I made that displeased him. But, being strong-willed myself and understanding my role as the parent, I would respond to his stubbornness and resistance with greater resolve not to cave. When Nathan would draw a line in the sand, I would step over the line and meet him eyeball-to-eyeball. Over time, he learned that he was not in charge. The funny thing is that when a parent (or any person in authority) feels that his or her authority is being challenged, the content of the discussion takes a back seat to the more pressing issue of who gets the last word. In those confrontations between Nathan and me, Nathan may in fact have been asking for something quite reasonable, but because of his angry attitude, I reacted negatively, rather than carefully evaluating the merits of his request.

> Unfortunately, many Christians feel that they need to approach their government leaders like a strong-willed child: angry, demanding, and proud.

But, smart lad that he is, as Nathan matured he gradually learned the secret of maximizing his ability to get what he wanted. He found that a respectful attitude and calm spirit worked much better than being boisterous and demanding. When Nate approached me with respect, my heart was much more open to listening to what he had to say, rather than just reacting to his contrarian spirit.

Unfortunately, many Christians feel that they need to approach their government leaders like a strong-willed child: angry, demanding, and proud. After all, we're right, and government *obviously* doesn't have a clue! The sad reality, however, is that such an approach is both contrary to Scripture and counterproductive in the long run.

In my six years running Michigan Family Forum, our staff discovered, refined, and used an approach to influencing legislation and policy that produced excellent results and, we believe, is consistent with wise scriptural principles. The crucial concepts of that approach are *prayer, piety, and persuasion.*

Prayer

We discussed the importance of prayer for governmental leaders in chapter 2. But the importance of prayer in enabling Christians to influence government doesn't stop there.

In working through normal marital communication issues, in raising children, in simply living a godly life in this world, we desperately need God's help. The avenue to entreat God is prayer. As we attempt to influence public policy, we need to bathe our efforts in prayer. Prayer can help us find favor with those in charge, as did biblical figures like Joseph, Daniel, and Esther. Prayer also helps us cultivate the right attitudes as we approach our leaders.

At Michigan Family Forum, to make prayer for our leaders more organized, we established the Michigan Prayer Network, which sought volunteers to pray for the specific needs of each state representative and senator and executive branch leaders. We forbade the prayer network volunteers to do any lobbying — they existed exclusively to pray for their assigned leader, as well as the leader's family and staff. We heard many thrilling reports of answered prayer, and I think we sent a good message to these leaders about our appreciation for them. We also had Christian school classes and homeschool groups "adopting" specific leaders for prayer. Often these leaders would visit the groups of children that had adopted them, opening up good relationships between youth and leaders that I'm confident left a lasting impression on both.

Soon after we'd started the prayer network, the news media chose to do a story about it. We were fearful that the media portrayal of our network would be negative, which might discourage legislators from cooperating with the volunteers. I expressed that concern to Detroit *Free Press* reporter Dawson Bell. And in the end, although his article did take a few pokes at us, its approach overall was calming and accepting. It quoted, among others, Howard Simon, executive director of our state's ACLU, whom I mentioned in chapter 2. His take on the prayer network was that it was probably "harmless" since no lobbying was being done. "In fact," he added, "if you know the legislature like I do, you'd realize they need all the help they can get!" Thank you, Howard!

Our government leaders do need prayer. So many times in the history of our nation, it was earnest prayer by our people crying out to almighty God that brought about huge victories. I love the story of the time, after the Revolutionary War, when our leaders at the Constitutional Convention in Philadelphia were debating what form our new government should take. Reaching a point of deadlock among the delegates, the least religious of all the framers, eighty-one-year-old Benjamin Franklin, rose to address those in attendance:

> In the beginning of the contest with Britain, when we were sensible of danger, we had daily prayers in this room for Divine protection. Our prayers, Sir, were heard and they were graciously answered. All of us who were engaged in the struggle must have observed frequent instances of a superintending Providence in our favor.... And have we now for-

gotten this powerful Friend? Or do we imagine we no longer need His assistance? I have lived, Sir, a long time, and the longer I live, the more convincing proofs I see of this truth: 'that God governs in the affairs of man.' And if a sparrow cannot fall to the ground without His notice, is it probable that an empire can rise without His aid? We have been assured, Sir, in the Sacred Writings that except the Lord build the house, they labor in vain that build it. I firmly believe this. I also believe that, without His concurring aid, we shall succeed in this political building no better than the builders of Babel; we shall be divided by our little partial local interest; our projects will be confounded; and we ourselves shall become a reproach and a byword down to future ages. And what is worse, mankind may hereafter, from this unfortunate instance, despair of establishing government by human wisdom and leave it to chance, war, or conquest.

I therefore beg leave to move that, henceforth, prayers imploring the assistance of Heaven and its blessing on our deliberation be held in this assembly every morning before we proceed to business.*

During the very dark days of our Civil War, Abraham

---

*From the notes of James Madison of the Constitutional Convention, 1787.

Lincoln, in calling our nation to prayer, observed how we as a people had become arrogant:

> We have been the recipients of the choicest bounties of Heaven. We have been preserved, these many years, in peace and prosperity. We have grown in numbers, wealth and power, as no other nation has ever grown. But we have forgotten God. We have forgotten the gracious hand which preserved us in peace, and multiplied and enriched and strengthened us; and we have vainly imagined, in the deceitfulness of our hearts, that all these blessings were produced by some superior wisdom and virtue of our own. Intoxicated with unbroken success, we have become too self-sufficient to feel the necessity of redeeming and preserving grace, too proud to pray to the God that made us!*

As our brave men stormed the beaches of Normandy in 1944, President Franklin Roosevelt prayed:

> Almighty God: Our sons, pride of our nation, this day have set upon a mighty endeavor, a struggle to preserve our Republic, our religion, and our civilization, and to set free a suffering humanity. Lead

---

* "Proclamation Appointing a National Fast Day," March 30, 1863, *The Collected Works of Abraham Lincoln*, Roy P. Basler, ed.

them straight and true; give strength to their arms, stoutness to their hearts, steadfastness in their faith. They will need Thy blessings. Their road will be long and hard. For the enemy is strong. He may hurl back our forces. Success may not come with rushing speed, but we shall return again and again; and we know that by Thy grace, and by the righteousness of our cause, our sons will triumph.... [T]hese men are lately drawn from the ways of peace. They fight not for the lust of conquest. They fight to end conquest. They fight to liberate. They fight to let justice arise, and tolerance and goodwill among all Thy people. They yearn but for the end of battle, for their return to the haven of home. Some will never return. Embrace these, Father, and receive them, Thy heroic servants, into Thy kingdom. And for us at home — fathers, mothers, children, wives, sisters, and brothers of brave men overseas, whose thoughts and prayers are ever with them — help us, Almighty God, to rededicate ourselves in renewed faith in Thee in this hour of great sacrifice. Many people have urged that I call the nation into a single day of special prayer. But because the road is long and the desire is great, I ask that our people devote themselves in a continuance of prayer. As we rise to each new day, and again when each day is spent, let words of prayer be on our lips, invoking Thy help to our efforts.... And, O Lord, give us faith. Give us faith in Thee; faith in our sons; faith in each other; faith in our united crusade.... With Thy blessing, we shall prevail over the unholy forces of our enemy....

Thy will be done, Almighty God. Amen.*

It takes humility to admit we need God. Isn't it refreshing to hear our leaders humble themselves and seek help from what Franklin called our "powerful Friend"? Truly, almighty God has been the best friend America has ever had. We need to seek him and his blessing again in fervent prayer. If every follower of Christ would spend even five minutes a day praying for America's government, churches, and families to submit to God's rule in their lives, this could be the start of a mighty return to him, another Great Awakening. As we'll discuss in chapter 7, nothing else will be sufficient to save us as a people.

Piety

A senator was invited to speak to a group of people who were livid that prayer had been expelled from our public

---

* See http://www.humanevents.com/article.php?id=43805.

schools. This group had pored over reams of data that had convinced them that many of America's vexing problems developed subsequent to *Engel v. Vitale*, the 1962 Supreme Court decision ending school-sponsored prayer in our schools. The group felt that restoring prayer in public schools would reverse our nation's downward spiral.

After thanking the group for inviting him to speak, the senator said, "I have two questions for you dear folks. First, how many of you really want prayer put back in public schools?" Everyone in the room immediately raised his hand. Some raised them with fists clenched, so strong was their conviction.

"Second," the senator continued, "how many of you within the past twenty-four hours took time to pray with your own children in the privacy of your own homes?"

It was as if the air had been sucked out of the room. A few parents sheepishly raised their hands; the rest looked down, realizing with surprise and no small amount of guilt that a significant point had just been made.

"Hmmm," the senator mused. "Then how can you expect the government to do what you're not doing in your own homes?"

Good question. It is tempting to become outraged at our government for the sin in our land, but we need to first look in the mirror.

I was speaking one day to a state senator about divorce reform. "You know," he said, speaking of bills I was supporting in my role with Michigan Family Forum, "your bills would make a significant change to our laws in Michigan."

I acknowledged that he was right.

He added, "You should also be aware that government is more a *lagging* indicator of where the culture is than a *leading* indicator."

Again he was right. Laws — even Supreme Court decisions I consider to be outlandish — are in large part a reflection of where the culture is. And culture is a reflection of the condition of the church and families in America.

My actions and attitudes speak far more loudly to my children than the words I say. If, as a dad, I cut moral or legal corners in any area of my life, I should not be too surprised if my kids take my bad example a step further. If I cheat on my income taxes, I shouldn't be shocked if my child shoplifts. If I speak ill of my boss, I shouldn't be surprised if my child smarts off at his teacher. If I constantly overindulge in mood-altering prescription drugs to "feel better," I shouldn't be surprised when my child uses street drugs and alcohol to get a high.

If we followers of Christ are really the salt of our earth,

a light on a hill, we must accept our role in setting the standards of right in our nation. As in our role as parents, what we Christians do and what attitudes we project in relating to our culture speak more loudly than our words. We would love to place the blame elsewhere, but many of the problems in our culture are a result of we Christians sending very mixed signals by our lives and attitudes.

For example, we decry hard-core pornography. Yet how many of us tolerate incredibly objectionable content on TV? If, even ten years ago,

> "I have lived, Sir, a long time, and the longer I live, the more convincing proofs I see of this truth: 'that God governs in the affairs of man.' And if a sparrow cannot fall to the ground without His notice, is it probable that an empire can rise without His aid?"
> — Benjamin Franklin

we'd seen and heard the things now being funneled at the speed of light into our family rooms, we would have been scandalized. But because things change slowly, we have accommodated ourselves to lower and lower standards.

We live in a time of hooking up, a time of casual sex on our college and now even high-school campuses. But Christian young people are themselves justifying these behaviors and cohabiting without marriage in increasing numbers.

Divorce is rampant in society. But the percentage of divorces inside the church is as high as the percentage outside. The devastation to families — to children in particular — and to our nation is immeasurable.

Abortion occurs not because people love to kill the unborn, but because we worship sex as a culture and devalue the natural result of sexual union: a child created in the image of God. Where do Christians stand on this issue? I believe it's something like this: *We Christians essentially agree that children are a pain and an expensive burden to bear and raise; we also agree that sex is really important. So it makes sense to maximize sex and minimize kids. But, because we are "pro-life," we teach that if you get pregnant you're stuck!* This hypocritical, unbiblical mentality feeds abortion, rather than combats it.

Imagine how things would change if we could convince ourselves and those around us of the truth that children are an unmitigated blessing of almighty God and that raising them is one of the greatest privileges known to man. Abortion would end in a moment. You could have abortion clinics on every corner, and no one would use them. "Are you kidding? Have an abortion and kill this precious child? No way!"

Our culture's openness to homosexual relationships also has come as a result of misplaced priorities on sexual gratification. Sex is a great creation of God, but he intended it not as an end unto itself, but as a means to two other wonderful ends: deep marital communication and the propagation of children, both within the confines of heterosexual marriage. But Christians have bought into the world's viewpoint when they endorse the faulty premise that life without consistent sexual expression is a life only half-lived. So gays and lesbians can rightly argue that the context in which sex occurs shouldn't matter. And once you accept that, it's a short step to accepting same-sex marriage, not to mention other activities that are contrary to God's revealed truth.

Repentance needs to start with me, with you. Scripture says, "Righteousness exalts a nation, but sin is a reproach to any people" (Proverbs 14:34, ESV). If government is a lagging indicator of our culture, and culture is a lagging indicator of the church, it is little wonder that American government is on life support.

Dr. Erwin Lutzer of Moody Church in Chicago nailed it:

It's popular to blame the Supreme Court, the humanists, and radical feminists for our country's eroding

111

standards of decency and growing disrespect for human life. But the responsibility might more properly be laid at the feet of those who know the living God but have failed to influence society.

If we were few in number, we might evade the blame, but there are tens of thousands of evangelical congregations and several million born-again believers in America. Yet we continue to lose crucial battles. *Perhaps the church doesn't suffer for the sins of the world as much as the world suffers for the sins of the church.**

The only hope we have for survival as a nation is for God to graciously answer our prayer for revival. And that can only come as we humbly repent of our own waywardness, as we return to God's standards for living, and as we lovingly communicate his grace and truth to the needy world around us. I assure you that this "bubble up" activity will impact our culture and then indirectly our laws in ways that all our lobbying and politicking could never accomplish.

---

* "Who Will Rescue the Rescuers?" *Moody Monthly*, April 1986, 28–31, emphasis added.

Persuasion

Every other part of this book deals with *understanding* the dynamics of how government works best, and how that relates to the responsibilities of those of us who identify ourselves as Christians. In that sense, it is *theoretical — strategic.* What follows in the rest of this chapter is a change of pace. It addresses the specific ways we Christians can actively attempt to make our influence felt in the halls of power. Therefore, it's *practical.* It's *tactical,* rather than strategic.

After we pray for our nation and its leaders and in true piety repent of our ungodly attitudes, actions, and words, there are times we need to exercise our citizenship by communicating with our elected leaders about issues that are important to us, our families, and our nation. Perhaps you've never done this in the past. You should — it's part of the responsibility of being a shareholder in this country to stay informed, vote, and, at times, offer your input on legislation. Many people find it far easier to sit home and complain rather than to communicate. That is a mistake. Sharing your thoughts with your leaders in government is one way of seeking "the peace and prosperity of the city" we read about in Jeremiah 29.

Successful persuasion requires having the right *attitudes*, the right *information*, and the right *request*.

The Right Attitudes

One day in my tenure at Michigan Family Forum, a well-intentioned friend dropped by and gave each of us a T-shirt he had made specifically for "our side." Written on the front of each shirt in large blue letters were the words: "Pro-Life, Pro-Family, Pro-God. ANY QUESTIONS???"

That T-shirt is typical of the combative attitude of many ardent conservatives as they approach public policy issues. We think it our duty to be brazenly IN YOUR FACE! But, like our son Nathan when he was younger, we are unlikely to be successful in the long run with this bombastic strategy. Fortunately, the Bible has much to say on how to lobby with effectiveness.

Proverbs 25:15 is a great place to start: "Through *patience* a ruler can be persuaded, and a *gentle tongue* can break a bone" (emphasis added). This approach is mirrored in the New Testament:

> And the Lord's servant must not quarrel; instead, he must be *kind* to everyone, able to teach, not resentful. Those who oppose him he must *gently* instruct, in the hope that God will grant them repentance

leading them to a knowledge of the truth, and that they will come to their senses and escape from the trap of the devil, who has taken them captive to do his will.

(2 Timothy 2:24-26, emphasis added)

You would think that people taken captive by the devil himself would need spiritual commandoes wielding AK-47s to swoop in and rescue them. But this passage from 2 Timothy clearly teaches that our style must be characterized by kindness and gentleness. Jesus set the example by overcoming the power of sin, death, hell, and Satan by dying on the cross in love.

When a wise evangelist attempts to bring a drug addict or prostitute to Christ, he doesn't cram truth down the listener's throat. Rather, he gently draws that needy soul to the truth. This is the picture of good persuasion: drawing people to the truth.

So before you visit with a leader, pray for yourself, asking God's help in remaining calm and patient and in trusting God to do the rest. Put a genuine smile on your face. Ask that God's love will flow through you to this leader. Remember, God cares more about this leader's eternal soul than about his vote on a specific piece of legislation. Remember also that God is absolutely sovereign — he is not nervously pacing in heaven, biting his fingernails and wondering how all this will turn out. Nor should we, his followers.

If you are writing to the leader, devote the letter to one issue only and be respectful of his or her time. Speak from the heart, but also thank him for serving his constituents in this position. Do not use bullying tactics. Don't just copy a form letter and send it in; that approach has minimal impact compared to an original, thoughtful, and respectful letter from you.

The Right Information

I've seen faith-driven citizens unload stacks of inflammatory books and articles on a legislative leader's desk with great commotion for added effect. I've also seen well-meaning advocates shove graphic pornographic pictures into the faces of unsuspecting leaders in an attempt to shock them to *do something* about this scourge.

Your leader will seldom if ever take the time to read great quantities of material or watch long videos you might provide him. And don't try to cram truth down his throat machine-gun style. Draw him or her to the truth by calm, patient words and by uncluttered printed material that carefully explains your point of view. Keep in mind that a legislator's scarcest commodity is *time*. Honor that reality by adhering to the time schedule the leader has made available to you; if your time expires before your communication is complete, offer to continue at the leader's convenience.

Be prepared, so that you can make your point clearly, powerfully, and briefly. Consider rehearsing your presentation with others. If you are seeking to persuade the leader to introduce new legislation, try to have bills that have been adopted in other states as examples, bearing in mind that each state will need to make its own modifications to fit into its own unique legislative scheme. Understand that, if you're successful in persuading the legislator to promote the bill in question, they will have little time to do the homework required to write the bill or to defend and promote it. Be willing to do as much as is required of you in assisting them, rather than expecting them to do the work on a bill that was originally *your* idea.

The Right Request

At some point in your communication with a governmental official, you will need to make your pitch — to ask that official for what it is you want. You may want his vote on pending legislation. You may want him to sponsor some new legislation. Be prepared to spell out clearly what it is you are seeking and what the next step might be.

"Senator, we would like you to consider cosponsoring a bill on this subject that is being authored by Senator Smith. Would you be willing to do that?"

If the leader wants time to think about it, suggest, "May I get back with you or one of your staff members in a few days to see what your decision is?"

If the leader has a question that you cannot answer to his satisfaction, offer to research the information and provide it for him. And then follow through.

All of this is just good common sense. The key here, as in much of life, is the Golden Rule. Treat your leader as you would want to be treated if you were in his position.

Following these steps of *prayer, piety,* and *persuasion* will maximize your effectiveness as a change agent in your state and our nation, to the glory of God.

6

Transforming Welfare — a Triple Win

Now that we've discussed some of the essential components of civil society, and understand what our role is as citizens who want to make a difference, it's time to address America's biggest crisis of our time.

As I have been campaigning for U.S. Senate in Michigan, I typically will ask a crowd what they consider our most significant problem to be. Generally, everyone — regardless of age — agrees we are in desperate straits in our land. But I get a variety of opinions from people as to what they consider to be the *cause* of our desperation. Some mention corruption in Washington; others talk about illegal immigration. Still others will mention our tax system, the Federal Reserve, ObamaCare, excessive regulations, governmental unions, out-of-touch leaders, and the like. But the most common answer I hear is the one I am convinced is truly the house that is on fire in our country: our national debt. That is not to minimize those other issues — but when your house is on fire, you don't paint your front door or wash the windows.

Any American who listens to the news knows the numbers: We are now over $15 trillion in debt as I write this.* Last fiscal year, ending September 30, 2010, the debt was growing at the rate of $4 billion per day. But as of the start of the new fiscal year in October 2011, the federal government's debt is now growing at the rate of $6.5 billion per day! That translates to a debt growth of $76,000 *per second* 24/7/365! For every dollar the federal government spends, it borrows 42 cents, much of that from other nations like China.

Amounts like $15 trillion are so immense they're hard to grasp. Let's put that number into a context we can identify with. Thanks here to Dave Ramsey.† He compared our federal debt to a family with a household income

---

* For a depressing update on the current status of our debt, go to http:// www.usdebtclock.org/.

† See http://www.daveramsey.com/article/federal-budget-vs-household-budget-how-do-they-compare/lifeandmoney_budgeting.

of $55,000 per year — but which is actually spending $96,500 this year, putting $41,500 of new debt on credit cards. If that isn't bad enough, our hypothetical family already has credit-card debt of $366,000. So after adding the $41,500, they still have an income of only $55,000 and credit card debt of $407,500.

Imagine that you're the head of that household — how would those financials feel to you? Terrifying? Remember that feeling, because that's how our country's financials *should* feel to our leaders in Washington.

Our leaders seem to agree that our growing debt is a problem. But no one seems to know what to do about it. The onerous job of reducing the debt was given to a so-called "super committee" of twelve legislators in 2011, but it should come as a surprise to no one that they couldn't agree on spending reductions. Even if they had, their suggested reductions, which would have gone into effect over the next ten years, would have slowed the growth of debt by a miniscule amount, roughly equivalent to a rounding error.

We need to do something significant soon. We are currently paying about 2.5 percent interest on our loans, but the historical average of interest the U.S. pays is more like 5.7 percent. As our debt grows inexorably toward $17 trillion, and the interest rate grows, we will be required to pay $1 trillion per year *just in interest*! Game over. We cannot sustain that payment. Look long and hard at the chaos in Greece. That is our future.

To us citizens, it seems recklessly foolish that our leaders can't seem to do what all of us are forced to do every day: balance our household expenses by getting our spending into line with our income. There are, of course, factors that complicate our leaders' task — such as strong lobbying groups that care deeply about every line item in our federal budget, and these groups have their hooks into our leaders. Another factor is the expectation of citizens: we have moved to an entitlement mentality.

> Math is math. The day of reckoning is upon us. We have made decisions based on a misunderstanding of the way the universe is wired, rather than on absolute truth.

All of this is bad enough. But on top of our current dilemma, let's not forget that this $15 trillion is simply the debt on our balance sheet today. We also have an estimated $62 trillion in unfunded liabilities growing from expected expenses in Medicare, Medicaid, and Social Security. These are monies we will have to pay in the future, and we haven't set aside nearly enough to cover them. Unless we begin to take action soon, these programs, in a handful of years, will be insolvent.

How did we get here? How was it that we, the richest and strongest nation in the world, woke up one day and found ourselves in this predicament?

It obviously didn't happen in a day. Denial comes naturally to us humans. But math is math. The day of reckoning is upon us. We have made decisions based on a misunderstanding of the way the universe is wired, rather than on absolute truth. Let's examine that misunderstanding so we can learn how to extricate ourselves from this slavery of debt.

Our federal government has grown rapidly in recent years. Much of that growth has come through the expansion of federal debt. This "buy now, pay later" philosophy is consistent with what's called a Keynesian theory of economics (named after twentieth-century British economist John Maynard Keynes), wherein the economy is supposed to grow as government puts more dollars into circulation. Trouble is, studies of other nations have shown that debt eventually reaches a tipping point compared to the gross domestic product (GDP) of a nation. At that point, adding more governmental debt significantly impairs that nation's economy. Most economists would concur the U.S. is nearing that point.* The Bible says that the borrower is the servant of the lender. A sound, conservative fiscal policy, based on biblical principles, would be to eschew debt except for very exceptional circumstances like war. And when the war is completed, we should pay down our excessive debt quickly, as we were able to do after World War II when our troops came home and we no longer had the expense of waging an expensive war on both sides of the globe.

> How can we reduce the size of our federal government today? The first thing is to recognize which functions we actually need, and which are consistent with our Constitution.

How can we reduce the size of our federal government today? The first thing is to recognize which functions we actually need, and which are consistent with our Constitution — and begin to eliminate those that either aren't needed or are inconsistent with the Constitution. For starters, I believe this should include elimination of the Departments of Education and Energy and the Environ-

---

* For a scholarly discussion of this relationship between debt and economic growth, see http://en.wikipedia.org/wiki/United_States_public_debt.

mental Protection Agency. None of these functions are listed or even implied in the part of the Constitution that gives powers to Congress (Article 1, Section 8). Education for our children needs to be administered locally, or, at most, statewide, not through a command-and-control framework centrally controlled by the bureaucracy in Washington, D.C.*

The Department of Energy has shown its ineptitude with investments in numerous alternative energy companies, the most noteworthy in recent days being Solyndra, the solar panel manufacturing company that wasted over $500 million of federal funds before declaring bankruptcy in September, 2011. Government is a very poor predictor of success, and should leave business investment decisions to market forces. Its budget request for FY 2012 is $29.5 billion, an 11.8 percent increase from FY 2011! Not only is energy management not listed nor reasonably implied in our Constitution as a function for the federal government to perform, the Department is doing a poor and wasteful job as well.

The federal Environmental Protection Administration has proven to be a rogue agency that steals American jobs by hyperregulating one's use of private property. The

---

* See Charles Murray's excellent article on this issue at http://www.hillsdale .edu/news/imprimis/archive/issue.asp?year=2012&month=01.

Fifth Amendment to the Constitution directly states: "No person shall ... be deprived of life, liberty, or *property*, without due process of law; nor shall private property be taken for public use, without just compensation." I maintain that the EPA is taking property rights away from citizens without lawful authority and without just compensation.

In direct costs to taxpayers, EPA is small compared to other federal departments and agencies, costing us *only* $9 billion per year. But the impact of its policies exact a much heavier toll on our economy. Just one of the EPA's new proposed regulations, reducing the amounts of atmospheric ozone to absurdly small levels, would cost in excess of $1 trillion to implement.[*] Then there is their rule declaring carbon dioxide, the gas found in all our lungs as we breathe and in the sodas we drink, to be a dangerous pollutant. The cost of this is estimated in the multiple trillions of dollars in the coming years.[†] EPA regulations take their place among the myriad of other federal regulations that cost job creators an estimated $10,500 *per employee* per year.[‡] That translates into

---

[*] See http://www.usnews.com/opinion/blogs/on-energy/2011/08/25/epas-proposed-ozone-regulation-could-cost-1-trillion.

[†] See http://blog.heritage.org/2009/12/07/epa-formally-declares-co2-a-dangerous-pollutant/.

[‡] *World Magazine*, "Hiring on Hold," 9-24-11, 35.

unemployment — job creators are unable to expand due to excessive costs associated with complying with a growing labyrinth of regulations. While bureaucrats may feel smug that they are making the world somehow safer or more perfect, one needs to ask why the ultimate human price must be paid by the millions of men and women who are without work and unable to properly provide for their families. All the regulations in the world cannot make life pain-free nor risk-free. In its attempt to do so, the EPA in recent years has gone way over the line. In addition, the federal agency is unnecessary because each of the fifty states has its own state EPA-like entity that can do what is needed to ensure that businesses do their part to treat our environment with due care.

Still, because of opposition, it will be a tall order for Congress to eliminate even a single federal department. Major forces inside and outside the governmental bureaucracy will resist the effort. And, even if we can muster the necessary political capital to pull it off, the growth of our debt is still likely to be unsustainable in the long run due to rising interest expenses. So what is the answer for putting out the fire of debt?

First, we need to step back, look at the big picture, and consider how we got into the mess we're in. Simply tinkering with the margins won't fix things. When you look at the federal budgets over time, you can see how error has crept in like the proverbial camel's nose in the tent. The influence starts small, but eventually looms very large. Currently, 70 percent of our federal budget is devoted to "dependency" type programming, such as housing, health care and welfare, retirement benefits, higher education subsidies, and rural and agricultural services. That is a major increase from 1962, when the percentage of the federal budget going to dependency programming was only 28 percent of the budget.* Looking at it from another perspective, while national defense consumed 49 percent of our federal budget in 1962, it dropped to only 20 percent of the budget in 2011, while "human resources" (which includes education, training, employment, social services, health, Medicare, income security and Social Security) climbed from 29.6 percent of the total budget in 1962 to 65.7 percent in 2011. Our national priorities have changed markedly.

The fastest growing part of our federal budget in the past twenty years has been a segment of dependency spending called *means-tested welfare programming*. This is just a fancy term for the federal welfare system that gives benefits based on an individual's or family's income. It

---

* See http://www.heritage.org/research/reports/2012/02/2012-index-of-dependence-on-government.

actually includes a total of seventy-one separate federal programs scattered across thirteen different federal departments and agencies, providing resources to poor and low-income persons in the following categories: cash, food, housing, medical care, social services, child development and child care, jobs and job training, community development, and targeted federal education programs. Specific names for the larger of these programs include: Medicaid, the Maternal and Child Health Block Grant, Temporary Assistance for Needy Families (TANF), Supplemental Security Income (SSI), the Emergency Food Assistance Program (which administers food stamps), and the Women Infants and Children (WIC) food program.

Means-tested welfare programs were a very small part of the federal budget when they were first introduced, but they didn't stay small. While dependency programs including welfare had their start during FDR's presidency in the 1930s, their growth remained modest until it began accelerating in the 1960s.

At his inaugural speech in 1961, President John F. Kennedy captured in one sentence what I believe is vintage American thought that runs counter to the idea of the expansion of federal welfare programming — particularly those programs that would provide handouts to citizens who are capable of helping themselves. The memorable line from his address was, "Ask not what your country can do for you — ask what you can do for your country."

But even as Kennedy spoke these words, there was a growing movement of people who naively believed that the poor could be depended upon to give their best to their country even if they were passively living off government assistance. In accordance with this assumption, social planners in the 1960s envisioned the potential of actually eliminating poverty from our nation. Churches and religious charities that had been helping the poor for decades were making no headway. It was time to bring out the big guns!

A leading voice in those days was Michael Harrington, who authored *The Other America* in 1962. Harrington reasoned that poverty is purely an economic issue, that people are poor only because they don't have enough money: "The means are at hand to fulfill the age-old dream: poverty can now be abolished." President Lyndon Johnson agreed: "For the first time in our history, it is possible to conquer poverty." Spurred by this thinking, and desirous of building his Great Society, Johnson led our federal government in declaring War on Poverty in 1964.

The price tag to win this war? Robert Levine, in his a

book *The Poor Ye Need Not Have: Lessons from the War on Poverty* said,

> If we were to provide every last poor family and individual in the United States with enough income to bring them above the level of poverty, the required outlay would be less than $10 billion a year.*

To eliminate poverty in America on so little investment — what a bargain! So logical, so filled with common sense, and ... so wrong. In 1964, when the War on Poverty was launched, state and federal outlays were $8.2 billion. Adjusted for inflation in terms of 2008 dollars, this is an expenditure of $54.6 billion.

By 1988, the combined federal and state price tag to end poverty had grown to $100 billion per year (adjusted for inflation, this would be approximately $300 billion). Was that enough to get the job done? Ronald Reagan mentioned the issue in his State of the Union address that year: "My friends, some years ago, the Federal Government declared war on poverty, and poverty won." Speaking over the ensuing laughter, Reagan continued his criticism of this misguided war:

---

* Robert Levine, *The Poor Ye Need Not Have: Lessons from the War on Poverty*, (MIT Press, 1970), 6.

Today the Federal Government has 59 major welfare programs and spends more than $100 billion a year on them. What has all this money done? Well, too often it has only made poverty harder to escape. Federal welfare programs have created a massive social problem. With the best of intentions, government created a poverty trap that wreaks havoc on the very support system the poor need most to lift themselves out of poverty: the family. Dependency has become the one enduring heirloom, passed from one generation to the next, of too many fragmented families.

Failing to learn from the mistakes and missteps of the past, Washington simply decided to throw more of our money at the problem. Now the total budget for state and federal expenses in means-tested welfare is close to $1 trillion per year. Per-capita expenditures have grown over eight times what they were when the War on Poverty began in 1964. The Heritage Foundation has documented that all the major wars our nation has fought from the Revolutionary War to the present have cost taxpayers approximately $6.4 trillion. By comparison, the War on Poverty has cost in excess of $17 trillion. And what is our national debt today? Pushing north of $15 trillion. There is a relationship.

But can we at least be grateful that all the money we have spent has gone a long way toward eliminating poverty? Hardly. We have more poor today (46.2 million) and the highest percentage (6.7 percent of the U.S. population) of the poorest poor category (those with income at 50 percent or less of the poverty level) since the Census Bureau began to collect such data.

Plus, as Ronald Reagan said, we make people dependent on handouts — making poverty difficult to escape — and we damage the family unit in America. How? By saying a woman can get assistance if she has a child out of wedlock, and as long as Daddy is not there. We once thought we could replace Daddy with a check. We now know better. Fathers are crucial in raising children properly. Even so, not only our welfare system but also our tax system and even ObamaCare have their own marriage penalties. That must also change.

While it's not fair to blame welfare alone for the growth of single-parent homes, it certainly hasn't helped. And the facts are clear: When our nation declared war on poverty, births out of wedlock were approximately 6 percent of total births in America. Now the rate exceeds 40 percent: 4 of 10 children born in the U.S. are born to an unmarried woman. In Detroit and many other urban areas, the rate of births out of wedlock is 8 out of 10! Even if welfare is not the only cause of these tragic numbers, the reality is that having a child out of wedlock is the doorway to generational poverty. In fact, the Heritage Foundation has concluded that marriage drops the poverty rate for children by 82 percent as compared to children living with an unmarried parent.*

These are numbers. Let's talk lives. James L. Payne, blogging in *The Freeman* on this subject, refers to a 1998 investigative reporting article in the *New York Times* (February 9, 1998) for which reporter Michael Janofsky traveled to rural Appalachia to see the impact of the War on Poverty. His conclusion was that despite the federal government's pouring billions of dollars into the area "to help residents overcome the economic and psychological isolation caused by poverty and the rugged terrain," there was "ample evidence that money and countless programs have had only marginal effects on breaking a cycle of poverty and despair that continues throughout many parts of Appalachia." Quoting one resident, a Denise Hoffman, 46, "The war on poverty was the worst thing that ever happened to Appalachia.... It gave people a way to get by without having to do any work." More than 46 percent were living in poverty as defined by the federal govern-

---

* See http://www.heritage.org/research/commentary/2011/06/marriage-is-detroits-secret-weapon-against-child-poverty).

ment, and more than half of the adult population is illiterate. The senior high school class voted to adopt as their motto, "I came. I slept. I graduated."

People are more than economic units. They have souls that need to be challenged to become all they were meant to be. Along these lines, emblazoned on my memory is a young man who came into my office when I was a prosecuting attorney. "Welfare killed my mother," he said matter-of-factly.

"What?" I said.

"Welfare killed my mother. You see, Dad was already long gone, but before she got on welfare, my mother, my siblings, and I worked together to survive. It was hard, but we made it. Then my mother realized she could get on welfare. Now all she does is sit in front of the TV and eat. Welfare killed her."

Even President Franklin Roosevelt, the father of many governmental programs, spoke in 1935 of the dangers of government handouts on our citizenry:

Continued dependence upon relief induces a spiritual and moral disintegration fundamentally destructive to the national fibre. To dole out relief in this way is to administer a narcotic, a subtle destroyer of the human spirit.

Any government which guarantees that every citizen will have his needs met is a government destined to go bankrupt. This is why a number of our European allies are financially stressed: they have been poster children for the welfare state. America is going down the same road.

"There is a way that appears to be right, but in the end it leads to death" (Proverbs 14:12). This is true for individuals, for families, for churches and, yes, for governments as well. Our leaders, confident in their own ability to eliminate a condition that has existed since history's earliest days, launched America on a course that has fractured families, lured otherwise capable people to become dependent on government handouts, and brought our nation to the brink of bankruptcy. It's high time our current leaders broke through their denial, admitted the error of their ways, and took steps to reverse this downward slide.

In *The Tragedy of American Compassion*, Marvin Olasky chronicles the history of the welfare movement in America during the past two hundred years. Recounting the variety of ways in which our ancestors approached the subject of helping the poor, Olasky suggests that there are two schools of thought: *social Darwinism* on one extreme and *social universalism* on the other. Social

Darwinism is survival of the fittest: "Let the poor sink or swim." It offers them minimal if any assistance. Social universalism, on the other hand, holds that society should unconditionally meet the needs of the poor regardless of whether the poor are doing what they can for themselves.

Repudiating both extremes, Olasky points to many times and places in the history of America when Protestant, Catholic, and Jewish volunteers would fan out across an impoverished community and meet human needs with wisdom, courage, and love. One particularly busy time for charity workers in New York City occurred in the late 1800s during a time of rapid urbanization and extreme poverty, the likes of which we can only imagine. But in the midst of this misery, valiant charity workers found that there are seven principles that actually could accelerate the effort to move the poor out of their dire straits. Olasky calls these principles "seven seals of good philanthropic practice." In alphabetical order, they are:

- Affiliation
- Bonding
- Categorization
- Discernment
- Employment

- Freedom

- God

While each of these seals is important, one of the most critical is *discernment,* which is based on the conviction that not all the poor are deserving of assistance. Those like orphans, the aged, and the incurably ill were helped without expectation of further action on their part. But as part of the *categorization* and *discernment* seals, those capable of employment were given a "work test" — men were asked to chop wood for other poor people and women to sew clothing for the poor. If they wouldn't work, they wouldn't be given food to eat. To those who feel this is cruel, consider the New Testament exhortation: "For even when we were with you, we gave you this rule: 'If a man will not work, he shall not eat'" (2 Thessalonians 3:10).

The goal of the charity workers was to get the poor, as soon as possible, into employment that would lead to freedom. To stay dependent on handouts was considered a form of bondage: Olasky said that "Charity leaders and preachers frequently spoke of freedom and showed how dependency was merely slavery with a smiling mask" (Olasky, *Tragedy,* 112). Finally, since so much of pauperism has a spiritual source, the last seal — *God* — was also very important to charity workers. One charity magazine, the *Legal Aid Review,* said in its January 1904 issue, "True philanthropy must take into account spiritual as well as physical needs."

Olasky points out that both Christian and Jewish charity workers successfully promoted the spiritual side of life from their own religious perspectives.

How successful were these efforts without government largesse? I encourage you to read the thrilling accounts yourself from Olasky's book. But for just one testimonial, Olasky draws on the investigative work of Jacob Riis, author of *How the Other Half Lives* published in 1890. After seeing much misery, Riis concluded that:

New York is, I firmly believe, the most charitable city in the world. Nowhere is there so eager a readiness to help, when it is known that help is worthily wanted; nowhere are there such armies of devoted workers.

Riis described how one charity group over eight years raised "4,500 families out of the rut of pauperism into proud, if modest, independence, without alms." He noted that another "handful of noble women ... accomplished what no machinery of government availed to do. Sixty thousand children have been rescued by them from the streets" (Olasky, 100–101).

Why do we keep thinking that government with its strong bent toward social universalism will someday figure out how to do welfare right? It is the nature of government *not* to be good at categorization or discernment. And legally, government cannot promote the seventh seal: God. So let's get government out of the welfare business before we totally bankrupt America and wreck more lives and families!

Moving welfare out of the federal government will not be easy. Keeping it where it is serves the interest of legislators who favor big government. Also, there are tens of thousands of people currently working in the trillion-dollar welfare state "industry" who will fight to preserve it. And, of course, there will be the hue and cry from the millions of welfare recipients who will not be overjoyed to have their benefits reduced or eliminated. I can hear some religious leaders telling us that it is unloving and non-Christian for government to cut help to the poor.

> To simply view the poor as a class of people that should be pitied and then kept in a state of perpetual dependency is not loving.

We are commanded repeatedly in Scripture to help the poor. I get a blessing helping those in need. But I do *not* get the same blessing paying my taxes, especially when I pay them to a government that actually hurts the poor. We desperately need to transform the welfare system because we do love people and want each individual to be all that God made him or her to be. To simply view the poor as a class of people that should be pitied and then kept in a state of perpetual dependency is not loving. I firmly believe that so many of those who come from poverty, if appropriately challenged and given opportunities, will respond with incredible greatness and growth. To encourage much more of this is very loving.

Columnist and author Star Parker grew up as one of nine children in a family on welfare. In her excellent book, *Uncle Sam's Plantation: How Big Government Enslaves America's Poor and What We Can Do About It,* Parker recounts her experience and provides very strong arguments about setting the poor free by helping them own responsibility for their own lives. In a recent TV interview, Parker expressed the opinion that government should vacate the area of welfare altogether:

> This whole notion that we should have a war on poverty dismisses the fact that individuals have a role in their own lives.... I'm one who believes that government has no business in charity, that this is

for communities, for the private sector to help those who really cannot help themselves.*

History is replete with stories of how the underdog surprises everyone by coming in first place. I believe the cure for AIDS and cancer and the solutions to some of the knotty technological problems complicating our world's energy future may well be discovered by some urban youth with a background of poverty who has been written off by society. Take, for example, Dr. Ben Carson, award-winning pediatric neurosurgeon featured in the TNT film *Gifted Hands.* This is a brief summary of his life:

Benjamin S. Carson Sr., M.D., had a childhood dream of becoming a physician. But he grew up in a single-parent home in Detroit, with dire poverty, poor grades, a horrible temper and low self-esteem. While that appeared to preclude the realization of his dream, his mother, with only a third-grade education, challenged both of her sons to strive for excellence. Carson persevered, attended Yale University and University of Michigan Medical School, and today is a full professor of neurosurgery, oncology, plastic surgery and pediatrics at the Johns Hop-

---

* See http://www.urbancure.org/mbarticle.asp?id=112&t=Watch-Star-Parker-Government-should-have-no-role-in-welfare.

kins School of Medicine. He has directed pediatric neurosurgery at the Johns Hopkins Children's Center for nearly a quarter of a century.

Carson holds more than 50 honorary doctorate degrees. He is a member of the Alpha Omega Alpha Honor Medical Society, the Horatio Alger Society of Distinguished Americans and many other prestigious organizations. He sits on the board of directors of numerous organizations, including Kellogg Co., Costco Wholesale Corp. and the Academy of Achievement. He is also an Emeritus Fellow of the Yale Corp., the governing body of Yale University. He was appointed in 2004 by President George W. Bush to serve on the President's Council on Bioethics. He is a highly regarded motivational speaker who has addressed various audiences, from school systems and civic groups to corporations and the President's National Prayer Breakfast.

Carson's first three books — *Gifted Hands*, *THINK BIG* and *The Big Picture* — provide inspiration and insight for leading a successful life. His fourth book, *Take The Risk: Learning to Identify, Choose and Live With Acceptable Risk,* was released in early 2008. Carson has been married for more than 30 years to his wife, Candy, and is the father of three sons. His mother, Sonya Carson, who made all this possible, is alive and well.*

Was it a government program that drew the greatness out of Ben Carson? No, it was a mother who believed in him, it was his conversion to Christianity, and it was years of hard work that enabled him to become what he was designed to be. How many other Ben Carsons are there in the inner cities of our nation?

So, how do we get from where we are to where we need to be? How do we find a way to end the slavery the welfare state has produced?

I say there are no easy ways to get there. With nearly a trillion dollars per year being spent on the welfare state, weaning government from this monolith will be difficult. *But it must be done!* Our leadership in Washington must set an aggressive goal of moving government out of the welfare business entirely, and then begin to cut means-tested welfare benefits at least 10 percent across the board in the first year to signal to the nonprofit and charity community that changes are coming. In the second year, budgets should be cut 30 percent of the total; the same in

---

*From the TNT website promoting the movie about Carson: http://www.tnt .tv/stories/story/?oid=44661.

the third and fourth years until the federal government is out of this area entirely.

But how will the poor who have become dependent on government handouts survive? Let me answer it this way: The county in which I live (Kent County, Michigan) has a population of slightly more than 600,000. The food stamp budget for our county is $200,000,000 per year. That's right — $200 million every year. I've asked scores of people what would happen if the Bridge Cards (the name given to food stamps in Michigan) quit working. How many people would starve to death in Kent County over the next twelve months?" The answer, given by almost 100 percent of those I asked this question, is, "None." Why? Because we won't allow people to starve to death. The church will act like the church again. Neighbors and extended families will do what we were supposed to be doing all along. God's people will need to get out of the locker room and into the game. We'll explore this more in the next chapter.

There will, of course, be pitfalls to be avoided in that transition. Having myself been part of a church staff that helped the poor in our midst, I know firsthand that it is very easy to simply replace or augment a social-universalist government program with an equally social-universalist church or charity program. We need to follow the principles promulgated by the charity workers of prior generations to ensure we move the poor to freedom and not to dependency on us.

There have already been success stories. I have already seen in action one nongovernmental program that is a wonderful tool to reach communities with the sweet sounds of liberty, opportunity, and empowerment. Part of a private initiative of community development begun by a wonderful group of innovative and caring people in Grand Rapids, Michigan, this program is based on principles that have incredible potential to revolutionize our entire nation, one community at a time.

Many aspects of this program are truly inspiring, but the part that interests me the most is a successful effort to move welfare recipients to work. Twenty years ago, Fred Keller, CEO of Cascade Engineering in Grand Rapids, felt a strong desire to help the poor by offering them sustainable work. His first attempts flopped. But then he arranged to have the local Department of Human Services station a worker inside his plant to assist with that challenging transition from welfare to work. Little by little, his efforts paid off. After eight years of success, having moved over four hundred people from welfare to careers, Fred and his team are able to say that 63 percent of those who made the transition are still off welfare! Now, other nonprofit groups throughout our community are doing similar work using the principles of *social enterprise*, the generic term for using the power of business to accomplish a social end, in this case moving people from welfare dependency to sustainable work.

The system is totally private and self-sustaining. Key to its success is the nonprofit group that works with the business to equip them to accept employees who are more challenging than normal — and also works with the new employees to prepare them to meet the expectations of an employer. So much of what those of us who are already working take for granted — money management, showing up on time, responding to the authority of a boss, etc. — needs to be taught to many of those who have had little or no experience in the working world. To ensure that the transition goes as well as it can, the nonprofit follows each new employee for at least a year. To provide motivation, employees are required to sign a promissory note to the nonprofit for $3000 — $2000 in cash and $1000 in sweat equity. While the employees work at the business, they are paid their living wage, plus the business pays the nonprofit one dollar for each hour the employee works. After fifty weeks, the $2000 cash part of the promissory note is paid in full. The employee pays off the remaining $1000 by donating one hundred hours at $10 per hour to their community to help others make the transition they made.

This is a wonderful and effective model for community improvement. It emphasizes personal accountability, initiative, and empowerment. It can be, and needs to be, replicated everywhere. Together with the approach taken by the charity workers of a century ago described earlier in the chapter, programs like this can help us move America back to economic strength and empower millions of Americans who are now caught in the trap of dependency.

When we do the things discussed in this chapter, it's a win-win-win. Our nation wins by reducing the size and expense of government. The economy wins because we gain the economic strength of millions of additional Americans giving us their productivity and creativity. And the people who are freed from the enslavement of handouts win — we welcome them as full participants in this awesome experiment in liberty called America.

7

My Life for Your Life

TRUTH LIBERATES. LIES ENSLAVE AND ULTIMATELY kill. That is true for individuals, for families, and for nations.

My passion for writing this book flows from my deep desire for my beloved country America to return to its truthful foundations so that our citizens and their families can again enjoy God's gracious gifts of life, liberty, and the pursuit of happiness.

Moving back to truth and liberty will be neither easy nor cheap. Perhaps the most difficult requirement will be the need for us to swallow our pride and give up our self-sufficient arrogance. I am convinced that positive growth will occur only when we humbly seek and follow God's wise plan for individuals, families, and nations as set forth in the Bible.

While the previous sentence may send shivers up the spines of those who feel that modern life is far too sophisticated to be directed by a book written by ancient people in a pretechnological age , it really shouldn't. The more you read and study the Bible, the more you will see that, while it was written by ancient people, its truths are timeless because they were inspired by a timeless, wise, and loving God. His principles for successful living are as applicable today as they were thousands of years ago and will be thousands of years from now.

> I am convinced that positive growth will occur only when we humbly seek and follow God's wise plan for individuals, families, and nations as set forth in the Bible.

At its core, life is really quite simple. There really are only two ways for individuals to live: One is centering my life around me, and the other is centering my life around God. The first approach will lead me to believe that I and my fellow humans are smart and good enough on our own to find a way out of the mess we are in. The second approach requires that, in humility, I concede that my sinful heart blinds me to a clear view of reality so that any real solution to my dilemma can only come as I earnestly seek the help and guidance of almighty God.

These two divergent approaches to life have been around since time began. The prideful, "we can do this without God's help" attitude was demonstrated long ago in the biblical story of the Tower of Babel. Since then, man has repeatedly attempted to create for himself a utopian system whereby he, with his great mind and technology, can fashion a world of his own making where, in theory at least, everything performs flawlessly. The challenge comes in deciding *what the rules are* — for every system of civil society requires rules or intolerable anarchy will result. The God of the Bible comes with his set of principles for living. But when God is expelled, man has to come up with his own set of rules, his own moral code to live by and expect others to do the same. And that is much easier said than done. It is complicated by the fact that many fellow citizens may have their own unique moral code that differs from the one enacted into law. Arbitrary laws — especially those that seem to favor the ruling class — become a source of major societal irritation. But, to avoid anarchy, at the end of the day, someone has to make the rules. Without God, what happens is that the person with the biggest stick gets to make the rules his way — might makes right. Our founders would call this tyranny.

In marked contrast, the framers of our nation believed that there is no need for us to create our own rules for living, nor do we need to create our own rights. They have always existed, because they emanate from the Creator. Our role, then, as humans, is to seek out these principles and carefully weave them into the fabric of our lives, and the lives of our families and our nation.

There are many instances in which our framers and those who followed them referred to the Bible to make decisions about the structure and substance of our government. Let me give just two examples:

1. We have built into our Constitutional framework that the President of the United States must be "natural born citizen."* This requirement is directly related to Israel's rule for a king found in Deuteronomy 17:15, "[B]e sure to appoint over you the king the LORD your God chooses. He must be from among your own brothers. Do not place a foreigner over you, one who is not a brother Israelite."

2. We established the separation of powers by dividing the authority of our central government into three unique branches — judicial, legislative,

---

* U.S. Constitution, Article II, Section 1.

and executive. So where did this come from? No, not from the Trinity. The concept of three branches of our federal government comes directly from Isaiah 33:22, "For the LORD is our judge, the LORD is our lawgiver, the LORD is our king; it is he who will save us."

Because the framers humbly sought the truth and wisdom of God, they were able to establish a civil society that has never been matched by any other nation in the history of the world in terms of liberty, opportunity, and growth. They weren't just lucky; they were *blessed*. And through the years, America has indeed been richly blessed. While severely tried by war and natural disaster, our system has proven itself sufficiently robust for over two hundred years.

However, in recent years, as we have already recounted in this book, America has been on a downward spiral. Unemployment, explosive debt, economic lethargy, a growing dependent class of people, and growing numbers of births out of wedlock are some of the symptoms of this decay.

Leaders from the left (liberals or progressives) seek more government to fix our problems. While they may deny it, many in the right are also looking to Washington to solve our problems but in a way that is almost the mirror image of the left. The left says our problems can only be solved with *more* government, while the right says our problems can only be solved by *less* government — but in both cases Washington holds the keys. I am definitely in the conservative camp politically, but I am convinced that both the right and the left are missing the crucial point. *Government by itself does not have the power to fix our nation!*

> Government by itself does not have the power to fix our nation!

We have the governmental policies we have because our people essentially want these policies. One frustration expressed repeatedly by Tea Partiers is that they help get good, conservative men and women elected only to have these leaders fail to make any major changes in office. Pro-life Ronald Reagan was our president for eight years, yet legalized abortion remains the law of the land. We have abortion because, on balance, our nation wants it that way. Let me prove my point: If you ask one hundred random Americans whether they think it is good to intentionally kill unborn boys and girls, most of them would say no. But if you ask the same group if you think a woman who has an unplanned pregnancy should be forced to carry her pregnancy to term, most would also say no. This ambivalence has resulted in abortion on demand that the majority of citizens consider a necessary evil.

Prohibition was enacted by the Eighteenth Amendment in 1919. It didn't work because our culture didn't really want it — so the Twenty-First Amendment repealed prohibition in 1933. Our governmental system is not a dictatorship where rules can be forced upon an unwilling people. We have a constitutional republic, a government "of the people, by the people, for the people," whereby the opinions and lifestyles of every citizen have their cumulative impact on governmental policy. Chuck Colson put it this way:

> Politics has become so big, powerful and controlled by the special interests that the only way it's going to be reformed is the culture. And when you stop to think about it, politics is simply a reflection of the values of the culture. You change the culture, you will change the politics. If politics is sick, it means the culture is sick — and we Christians are responsible for the culture... I hope everybody gets involved, gets active and prays.*

As I have been campaigning for more than a year all

---

* See http://www.citizenlink.com/2010/08/27/friday-five-chuck-colson-on-religious-freedom-and-christian-citizenship-2/.

across the state of Michigan, I have spoken to thousands of people, many of whom fully realize the importance of making changes in our nation before America goes over the brink. These folks want change! And change is sorely needed. But I frequently give them a reality check: As capable and as passionate as I (and the other candidates) may be, don't think for a second that any one of us will go to Washington on our white horse and wave a magic wand over the Capitol building and single-handedly make it all better. The significant structural changes that are needed — some of which we have discussed in this book — will not happen unless the citizens of America have a change of *heart*. Right now, our giveaway welfare programs exist because people want them — they possess an entitlement attitude. Unless that attitude changes, we are heading for economic and cultural chaos that will impact us all and bring irreversible change to our nation.

So what is the answer? Chuck Colson said it: "Christians are responsible for the culture." We Christians have the truth of Scripture our nation so desperately needs. People need to not only hear the Word, but see it lived out in our lives. Let's face the facts: We have not been the salt to preserve our nation, and the light to guide and teach our fellow Americans. In the words of Erwin Lutzer, "The world suffers for the sins of the church." We people of

God need to start with *repentance*. That thought brings to mind the well-known scripture, 2 Chronicles 7:14:

> If *my people, who are called by my name,* will humble themselves and pray and seek my face and turn from their wicked ways, then I will hear from heaven, and I will forgive their sin and will heal their land.
>
> (emphasis added)

This scripture contains an incredible promise. If we will do four things, God promises to do three. Our responsibility is to:

- **Humble ourselves:** This is a voluntary action to put ourselves, as it says in the Pledge of Allegiance, "under God."

- **Pray:** The Hebrew means *to intercede.* This is an opportunity to pray for family, friends, neighbors, other citizens, and our leaders.

- **Seek God's face:** This is separate step from praying; the Hebrew means to repeatedly and urgently seek the very presence of almighty God.

- **Turn from our wicked ways:** This means to turn away from our sinful wandering and back to God and his ways.

If we do these things, God then promises to:

- **Hear from heaven:** God will pay attention to our prayers from his home in heaven.

- **Forgive our sins:** God will pardon our national and individual sins.

- **Heal our land:** God will bring restoration to our nation.

Just imagine what would happen if all the true followers of Christ in America would heed this scripture with sincerity. I am personally drawn to the huge challenge of Jesus who called us to "deny ourselves, take up our cross daily," and follow him. He added, "For whoever wants to save his life will lose it, but whoever loses his life for me will save it" (Luke 9:23–24).

Our culture is so self-centered. In effect, we daily communicate to those around us: "Your life for my life." In other words: "You sacrifice for *me*. *I'm* the important one here!" But Jesus came with a heart that said, "My life for *your* life. I give myself freely for you." Imagine if every blood-bought follower of Christ would imitate our Leader and demonstrate to his or her neighbors, friends, and even enemies: "My life for your life." This is how the early church turned the Roman world upside down, with men and women willing to suffer loss of property and life itself for the sake of those who didn't know him. This is how our brothers and sisters in other nations today are impacting their worlds for him. I'm told that the provinces in China where the church is growing the fastest are also the provinces where the church is under the greatest governmental opposition. Do we need to come under more severe persecution in America for the church here to genuinely follow Christ? What would it take for us *now* to courageously step out of our comfort zones daily and give of ourselves to those around us who need to know him and follow him?

> I'm told that the provinces in China where the church is growing the fastest are also the provinces where the church is under the greatest governmental opposition. Do we need to come under more severe persecution in America for the church here to genuinely follow Christ?

Does this sound too difficult? Do you feel intimidated by the opposition? Join the club. But then meditate on the words of our King:

> *All authority* in heaven and on earth has been given to me. *Therefore* go and make disciples of all nations, baptizing them in the name of the Father and of the Son and of the Holy Spirit, and teaching them to

obey everything I have commanded you. *And surely
I am with you always, to the very end of the age.*

(Matthew 28:18–20, emphasis added)

Paul told us in Romans 8 that, while persecuted, we
are "more than conquerors." Any attempt to hurt us only
makes our movement more impactful because none of us
can overrule the sovereignty and love of God.

So, Christian, what is your next step?

In our campaign for U.S. Senate, God has shown us
something that many are finding helpful. It all started
when I decided not to take Political Action Committee
(PAC) money from corporate or trade association PACs.
While legal, I consider it unseemly at best, and legalized
bribery at worst. But, in place of this, we have formed a
Healing America PACT that contains the heart of what
I believe will change our nation. The guidelines for each
person who joins the PACT are:

- **Pray.** Not just a casual "God bless America,"
  like politicians like to tack onto the end of their
  speeches —something like sprinkling pixie dust
  over our country with some magical incantation.
  I'm talking about daily, earnest prayer, both by
  yourself and, whenever possible, with others —not
  only those from your congregation, but if possible,

other groups throughout your city. What should we pray for? Our leaders, our families, and that true followers of Christ in America will *be* the church 24/7/365. To be part of the Healing America PACT, commit to praying daily for another Great Awakening in America like those that brought our nation back to him in previous generations. America is on life-support spiritually and needs an infusion of God's righteousness in our individuals, families, and nation. Prayer alone, and the actions that prayer sparks, are essential to ignite this spiritually healing fire.

- **Ask God what he wants you to do.** Asking God this question implies that we desire Christ to be Lord of our lives every day, to daily take up our cross and follow him in the routine of life. And beyond the routine, who knows what major life changes God may have in store for you? God does have plans for us. But are we listening? I love the scripture that says, "For when David had served God's purpose in his own generation, he fell asleep" (Acts 13:36). Despite huge personal failures at times, the net impact of David's life was that he fulfilled God's purpose for him in his generation. Will you? Will I? Other scriptures talk about God's plans for his people. See Jeremiah 1:5; Galatians 1:15-16; Ephesians 2:10. Ask God for wisdom with a heart that is willing to do *anything* he asks, and he will give it to you (James 1:5).

- **Courageously obey.** Are you willing to get out of the comfort zone you've been living in and do something outrageous for him if he clearly leads you to do so? Be careful —if you say *yes*, this choice may lead you to travel to an inner city and minister to the needs of children and families impacted by poverty. It may result in you traveling to other parts of the world as a missionary, bringing the Gospel to those in need. It may lead you to run for public office. The key here is to listen to God, get godly counsel, stay in the Word and, when he speaks, take the first step of obedience. See then if he doesn't open another door of opportunity. Listen to the godly counsel of others, but take don't let what Dr. Bruce Wilkinson called the "Border Bullies" talk you out of what you know God has shown you to do. These bullies are well-meaning people who have forgotten how, with God, all things are possible. They are the ones who are quick to say, "You can't do that! Who do you think you are? You're not qualified —and even if you were, it's impossible!" Instead, take that first step and see if God doesn't open more doors. God is always in the business of doing the impossible and getting the glory for it. It's about him, not us. And remember: obedience applies to major decisions, yes, but also the normal, the routine, the mundane. The Christian life is a "long obedience in the same direction." To be part of the Healing America PACT, you choose to obey him throughout your day, in the big and small decisions. And when (not if!) you fail, you confess, repent. and get back on your horse and go on.

- **Together.** We need to see ourselves as part of what God is doing in and through all our nation's citizens. I challenge you to become part of the Healing America PACT by going to http://randyhekman2012.com/PACT and joining with others. Let's be part of what God is doing to bring healing back to our nation through his people seeking to live the truth in their lives on a daily basis.

America is at the Crossroads. Will we continue down the road toward economic and spiritual oblivion? Or will we rouse ourselves and take a stand against the trends of

> There really are only two ways for individuals to live: One is centering my life around me, and the other is centering my life around God.

our day? Will the followers of God rise up, cry out to him daily for the next Great Awakening, and choose to courageously live righteous lives for his glory in these exciting days?

If each of us does our part with fervent prayer and appropriate action, we believe God will bring healing to our nation. Let's act while we still have the freedom to do so!

About the Author

Randy Hekman, who lives with his wife, Marcia, in Grand Rapids, Michigan, is running for the U.S. Senate.

A U.S. Navy veteran and former prosecuting attorney, Randy became, at age twenty-seven, the youngest judge elected to the bench in Michigan. While he held the judgeship, Randy wrote a book, *Justice for the Unborn*. Inspired by a case he had presided over, it is still widely read and is regarded as the quintessential go-to book on the unconstitutionality of abortion.

After serving for fifteen years (with two uncontested reelections) as a judge, Randy voluntarily left the bench to start Michigan Family Forum, a family policy council advocating for family issues. MFF is associated with Focus on the Family. Building that organization from the ground up, Randy and his team during his six years there helped impact the charter school movement and other issues that affect the family in the state of Michigan. After his departure from MFF, Randy served as executive director of CBH Ministries and then executive pastor of Crossroads Bible Church in Grand Rapids.

Randy and Marcia are the parents of twelve children (all successfully raised) and grandparents of twenty-two!

In March of 2011, Randy and Marcia sensed a strong call from God to run for the U.S. Senate seat currently held by Democrat Debbie Stabenow. Randy is well aware that *the strength of a nation does not flow down from its government, but up from the character of its people.* In running for public office, Randy has been able to use his "bully pulpit" to communicate truth to a large audience. His purpose is to bring much-needed healing to America. This will remain Randy's top goal after his election to the Senate.

A Special Note
from the Author's Wife

I HOPE YOUR HEART HAS BEEN TOUCHED BY THIS BOOK that Randy wrote to bring healing to our hurting nation. I also hope you are motivated to join the Healing America PACT. And I hope that you will follow Randy's urging to pray daily for our nation. But some of you may be confused about what to include in those prayers.

As a young person, I tried to pray daily and even read the Bible, but I just couldn't stick with it. Then, in college, a friend shared with me how she actually knew Christ in a real and personal way. Jesus' words in Revelation 3:20 spoke to me: "Here I am! I stand at the door and knock. If anyone hears my voice and opens the door, I will come in and eat with him, and he with me." That means that we can have a very close, intimate relationship with him if we invite him into our hearts. I prayed a prayer like this:

> Lord Jesus, forgive my sins. I open the door of my heart and life to you and receive you as my Savior and Lord. Please take control of my life and make me the person that you want me to be. Thank you for dying on the cross for me and for coming into my heart as you promised.

He came into my heart and promised to never leave me nor forsake me (Hebrews 13:5). If you have never received Christ into your heart, I encourage you to pray that prayer. When you do, you will become his child, and he will begin to work in your life in amazing ways, including helping you do your part to bring healing to America.

Please let me know if you did pray that prayer for the first time, and we will send you some helpful steps on how to grow in your relationship with Christ. It is exciting to be on this journey together!

Marcia

Email me at: Marcia@healing-america.org

or write me at: 678 Front Ave NW, Suite 177,
Grand Rapids, MI 49504